Praise for *Two Liv*

"Glenn surprises you at how adept one can be while conceal-ing the fact that he is different. I had no idea that dyslexia affects day-to-day life in such enormous ways. Glenn, with Melva by his side, has led an amazing life by overcoming struggles with abilities that most of us take for granted. I love happy endings."

> — Donna Ready, events promoter,
> Village of Grand Lake, Colorado

"My wife JoAnn and I have known Glenn Harrington for over 20 years now, and I had the joy of being his pastor for much of that time. Seldom have I been around a man who gets so much out of life and in return always finds a way to give so much back. Somehow I always had this strange feeling that there was a dimension to Glenn that went much deeper than whatever it was we happened to be involved in together at any given time, but he and Melva are both so engaging that we always seemed to get lost in the moment whenever we were with them. We count them among our dearest friends, and having read Glenn's incredible story, we understand even better just what a treasure our relationship with them has been."

> — Jim Weber, president, Global Connection
> International

Two Lives in One

The Struggles and Triumphs of a Dyslexic Mensa

GLENN HARRINGTON

With Faith Marcovecchio

Two Lives in One: The Struggles and Triumphs of a Dyslexic Mensa
by Glenn Harrington
with Faith Marcovecchio

Published by:
Glenn Harrington

Book Design: Nick Zelinger, NZ Graphics

ISBN: 978-0-615-75760-5

Library of Congress Control Number: 9780615757605

First Edition

Printed in the United States of America

Dedication

This book is dedicated to my wife, Melva, and our three daughters, Beth Marie (deceased 1994), Marsha Kay, and Tina Gale.

I still feel it is important for Melva to be proud of me, and I still enjoy making her laugh and showing off in front of her even though we have been married for over sixty-one years.

We two are truly one. (Matthew 19:5)

I have always enjoyed the support and encouragement of our three daughters, even though as pre-teenagers they could not understand why Daddy had to ask Mother how to spell simple words they knew how to spell.

The greatest traveling partner a man could have in this journey of life is a wife like Melva. Without her gentle encouragement and patience, this book and this journey would not have been possible, and surely the destination would have been different.

Contents

Preface

Most people know me as Glenn, but that is only my name, only a string of letters. Unless you can put them together and read them within the context of my life, you cannot truly know who I am. Those letters, my name, don't allow you to look inside me and see my greatest accomplishments or my most difficult challenges. They don't explain the wonderful or hurtful events I have gone through. They don't tell you about the loving people in my life or the ones who turned away from me when I needed them most.

Words, like the letters that form my name, have always held a place of power and mystery in my life. That is because I am severely dyslexic, and will never be able to read beyond the fourth-grade level.

Today there are ways of detecting dyslexia and helping the children and adults who face the challenges of this neurological disorder. But I was born in a time before dyslexia was understood or even recognized. When I grew up in the thirties and forties, children who struggled with reading and writing were labeled lazy or dumb. Teachers and other adults provided little help to boys and girls who avoided reading aloud, handed in writing assignments filled with misspellings and covered in eraser marks, and labored to turn in a test before class time was over.

The silence I faced in response to my struggle with written words forced me to adapt. I learned how to hide my poor reading skills. I discovered the importance of an outgoing personality and being polite. And I focused on the things I could do well, like visualizing how the parts of an engine work together, or seeing in my mind's eye how I could run my coach's plays on the football field, or knowing how to survive in the wilderness with just the few things I carried on my back. But not being able to read and spell like everyone else also made me feel there was something wrong with me, something I couldn't talk about or ever hope to overcome.

It took the love of my wife and my belief in myself to push beyond those fears and attempt to do things that as a child, I never thought I was capable of. I went to college, became a teacher, and earned a master's degree. I worked as a naturalist for the National Park Service, served in local government, and at age 76, became a member of the American Mensa society. For people who don't experience the challenges of dyslexia, it's hard to understand what it means to accomplish such things. But consider this: I have never read a book. I cannot spell many words without the help of my computer. I never write in front of others. And I still don't read aloud.

And yet, I am a firm believer in the healing power of paper and pen. As difficult and time consuming as it is for me to sit in front of my computer and put words on the screen, writing allows me to revisit parts of my life in order to understand the gifts I have been given and the influence remarkable people have had on me. By publishing my story, I can allow others to look inside my heart and mind. I hope that my words can help anyone who struggles with life's challenges, especially dyslexics, to gain self-confidence as I have and live an equally rich and rewarding life.

As strange as it may sound, I consider being dyslexic a gift, not a handicap. It has given me a life filled with joy and the blessings of three daughters and a wife who is truly a part of me. It gave me a profession I loved and feel I was born to pursue: teaching. And it challenged me to reach higher and farther than I thought I could ever go, especially as a young child struggling with words on a page.

Acknowledgments

This book would not have been possible without Mr. Rex Ryan. A professor at Midwestern University, he saw to it that I finished my undergraduate work, and he was the only person who ever tried to help me learn to read. Although he did not help me write this book, I felt he was looking over my shoulder, guiding me through the process and seeing that I finished.

I would also like to thank Faith Marcovecchio, who spent countless hours editing the manuscript. Her talent to decipher my thoughts, capture the feelings I wanted to convey, and present the material I gave her brought the story to life.

Mark Graham, a writer, publisher, and friend, guided me through publishing this book. With his understanding of my needs and his patience with my confusion, he was able to lead me gently to the final product.

"It takes more than just a writer to produce a finished book."

CHAPTER 1

Foreigner in a Native Land

When I was a little boy, two of my uncles gave me nicknames. Uncle Bradley called me the Frenchman, and Uncle Skeet called me the Chinaman. It wasn't because I had a debonair grin or almond-shaped eyes. They labeled me a foreigner because most of what came out of my mouth sounded like the language from a faraway land.

It was the early 1930s, and we lived in Baytown, Texas. The Depression was on and my father was working as a boiler plant operator at Humble Oil and Refinery. As the economy continued to grind America to a halt, the refinery prepared to lay many of the men off. But our family got lucky. Humble offered my father a job in the Two-Bit Labor Gang, earning twenty-five cents an hour for cutting grass, digging ditches, and doing other menial work. Lucky, of course, was relative.

Those were hard times, but we got by. Dad also brought in income by preaching on the weekends. In return for his work on the pulpit, my father accepted offerings from the congregation each Sunday. Then, when I was three, we moved out to the country, where we could have a cow, some chickens, and a garden—another way to make ends meet. Mother, like most women of the time, was a homemaker and a great saver. One of her treasures was a large set of glass canning jars that she used to preserve the vegetables we grew in our garden and meat from calves we raised and butchered.

I was the youngest of three boys. My two brothers, Raleigh and Happy, were several years my senior. They were Dad's favorites, and took advantage of their position in the family to tease and bully me, about my garbled speech and everything else. Left to fend for myself, I soon learned that my best defense was escape, and so the pastures and woods around our place in the country became my closest allies and dearest friends. I spent many hours on my own building forts and tree houses, hiding out from imaginary Indians, and skipping stones or building miniature rafts to float on the pond near our house. As I grew older I learned to hunt and fish, and would often head out on my own for days at a time to explore the countryside near the shores of Galveston Bay and camp out under the stars.

Those times, though lonely, gave me two things that would forever enrich my life: a love of nature and a rich imagination. Throughout my time on this earth, wilderness and a creative mind have been both my greatest escapes and the places where I find my truest self. In childhood, whenever I felt isolated or alone, I knew I could disappear into the woods or my imagination and find peace, contentment, and a sense of mastery there.

* * *

It wasn't until I began school that I realized I was different from the other children. Socially, I did fine. I had craved friendships during my years alone as a small boy, and going to first grade expanded my world tremendously. Before long I had a large circle of friends at Ashbel Smith Elementary. For a boy who had always been left out of things, I finally felt accepted. At recess, lunch, and on my long walk home, I was the center of a happy group of boys and girls, enjoying every minute of it.

Yet it wasn't long before the difficulty I'd had learning to talk reasserted itself with written language. My schoolwork, especially reading, spelling, and writing, was challenging and terribly frustrating—especially for a boy who was otherwise bright and engaged. First grade passed, then second, and I still couldn't read. It wasn't until third grade that I finally started recognizing words on a page, and even then they never seemed to stick. Though my memory was good, I couldn't hold on to sequences of letters. I might be able to spell or read a word one day, but a few days later it would be gone. Looking around, I marveled at how easily the other children seemed to master what for me was an almost impossible task.

I knew this was a problem I needed to hide, so I figured out ways to cover my tracks. Ironically, my little white lies first appeared at church.

Some of our relatives had helped my father build a small Assembly of God Church and establish a congregation in a nearby town. Dad's nickname was Preacher, and he and my mother raised us boys to be good, solid Christian men for whom going to church every Sunday was never an option. As the preacher's sons, we needed to know our Bibles and our hymns. And to all the people sitting in the pews around my family, it appeared that I did. When Dad told us to turn to a specific verse, I'd be the first one there, meeting his eyes with a smile over my Bible. But the truth was, I'd be nowhere near whatever verse he'd named. I was faking, a technique I developed into an art as a child—and even more so as an adult.

Singing hymns was a second test of my ingenuity. My reading was so slow that I simply couldn't keep up with the music. At first I'd move my lips as though I was singing, but that wasn't foolproof enough. So I figured out a new tack: I started to hum instead. It wasn't that I couldn't carry a tune; I just couldn't follow the words in the hymnal. I knew I'd hit on something good when the people around me started humming too. Before long it became a hallmark of our little church that many members of the congregation hummed instead of singing their hymns.

Faking my way through readings and hymns turned out to be pretty easy. The biggest challenge of all came during Sunday school. In class, each of the children would be asked to read a Bible verse or two. Suddenly, my white lies were forced to grow. When the teacher called my turn, I'd find an excuse or suddenly have to go to the restroom. Somehow, week in and week out, I managed to avoid the dreaded task. I was always polite to the teacher, always apologetic with my excuse, but absolutely determined that I would not humiliate myself by reading aloud in front of others.

It may seem that all these pretenses and excuses were in conflict with my Christian upbringing, but I didn't see it that way. For me, my tricks were a matter of survival. I did what

I needed to do as a poor reader in a world of words. In order to hide my humiliation and emotional pain, I pretended to be like everybody else.

CHAPTER 2

One Page
Before the Bell

Though more than sixty years have passed since those five short words rang in my ears, the thought of them still makes my stomach drop: One page before the bell.

By the time I got to fourth grade, I thought I had become good at hiding my poor reading. In school as in church, most people didn't seem to know how bad my problem was. They saw me as a happy kid with lots of friends, polite to my elders and respectful of authority. I understood some subjects in school, such as math and science, and as long as no reading was involved I could grasp the concepts and remember them. But anything that required reading or writing was a different story. A short writing assignment that might be easy for others was for me the cause of great, stomach-twisting anguish.

Unfortunately, one of my teachers loved to have us write at the end of the hour. "One page before the bell," she would call out to my dismay. Most of the time I knew the subject we had been assigned and could talk about it easily. But writing about it was an entirely different matter.

Being near the Gulf, it was hot and humid in our classroom almost year-round, and in the 1940s we didn't have the luxury of air conditioning to cool us off. The sweat already forming on my brow would start to flow as children got out their paper and pencils. I would write, erase, rewrite. I gripped the pencil so hard that my hand hurt, and sometimes I would bite my knuckles just to distract myself from the emotional pain. It didn't help. The letters were simply not forming words. Nothing was fitting together.

I'd keep working, biting the soft metal around the eraser on my new pencil to push out the little that was left. Time was almost up. My page was worn with holes from over-erasing, messy with smudged lead. The bell was about to ring, and as usual I was the last student to turn my paper in.

As I approached the teacher's desk, my eyes would be glued to the floor. Shame overwhelmed me, but I couldn't let anyone see. I'd catch her eye as I handed over the assignment, watch her scan the sloppy page, frown with disgust, and turn away.

This happened over and over, day after day. The teachers must have known I couldn't spell or write well, and yet I don't remember any teacher ever asking me about it, ever giving me special help with my writing or reading.

Instead, they allowed me to struggle alone, treating me like I was any other kid. I was different and nobody noticed. And the disappointment of being ignored was almost worse than the problem that so desperately needed attention.

* * *

Because I was well-liked, the other students tried to help me, to the limited extent that they could. In reading class, we often had to stand and read aloud from our textbooks. The teacher would start at the front of the first row, move down that row and up the next, and continue on until everyone had a chance to read. Because my last name begins with H, I always had a little time to prepare before she got to me.

First I'd count heads, then paragraphs in the book, settling on the passage that would be mine. I'd scan it for long words, whispering to the students around me for help. When it came my turn to read, I was as ready as I could ever hope to be. But as the reading traveled down the row of desks, the knot in my stomach grew, and I realized there could never be enough time to prepare for this painful exercise.

Students never teased me openly about my reading, but it was always embarrassing when I couldn't pronounce a word. My heart would race, my lips would get dry, and I'd feel the hot flush of disgrace on my face and neck. I'd flash my eyes around the class and manage a little smile, mumble words in the hope that no one could tell if I said them correctly or not. Often someone would giggle or say the word loud enough for me to hear, but it was always embarrassing. After three or four failed attempts to make it through my paragraph, I'd be devastated. If I'd had any desire to read at the beginning of the school year, the feeling was long gone by the end of my first humiliating day.

By the end of the fourth grade, it looked like my reading charade was up. The teacher gave me a note to take home to my parents and told me what it said. I was going to be retained and would have to repeat the fourth grade.

I stuffed the note in my pocket and threw it away as I walked home that afternoon.

A few days passed, and the teacher called me up to her desk. Had I given the note to my mother and father? "Yes," I lied. Several more days went by, and because she hadn't heard from my parents, she pulled me aside again. For some reason, she'd decided to cut me a deal. Did I think I could try to do better if they let me go up to the fifth grade? she asked. "Yes," I lied again. And so I was allowed to pass to the fifth grade "under conditions," meaning that if I didn't do better at the beginning of fifth grade, I'd be put back to the fourth.

I didn't do better, but the subject was never brought up again. I was a quiet little boy, a good child who was never a discipline problem, and because I never demanded any special attention, I was never given any. The teacher thought she had done me a favor by passing me along. In reality I needed someone to say something, anything, to let me know they knew my terrible secret and would help me learn to read.

* * *

In the spring of 1943, at the end of my fifth-grade year, the teacher announced that we were going to have a reading contest. Whoever read the most collective pages over the next four weeks would win a very special book.

Neither the prize nor the contest interested me in the least. I didn't want a book because I didn't read books, and besides, I could never compete with the other children in my class, who by that time were reading full-length adventure stories about characters like Tarzan and the Black Stallion.

24

But as the contest date approached, my friends started talking about who would win. Soon the excitement of the other boys and girls pulled me in. I wanted to be a part of the class whether I was a good reader or not. But how could I be?

Then, during recess one day, I figured it out. I started talking to a friend of mine whom I knew had read a thick book called *Little Women*. I asked him what it was about. Before the bell rang, he told me everything he could remember. A light went on inside my head, and I stored the story away.

That afternoon I checked *Little Women* out from our school library. It sat next to my bed for a few days unopened before I brought it back to school and returned it. I had a plan. Now I was ready.

To prove we had actually read the books we were listing for the contest, each student had to meet with the teacher and provide an oral summary of the plot and characters. I spent twenty minutes with Mrs. Grant telling her everything I could remember from my friend on the playground. She nodded and smiled, then wrote down the number of pages in *Little Women* next to my name. I was elated. I had never felt so good about schoolwork in my entire life! So I did it again, then several times more. At the end of the contest, when the teacher added up the pages each student had reportedly read, I was shocked to discover that I had the most.

Mrs. Grant called me to the front of the class on the day the prize was handed out and ceremoniously presented me with my special book. On the title page was an inscription.

Though I never broke the binding, I kept that book for many years. It made me feel important in front of my friends. They finally thought I could read.

As important as that day was for me, though, it didn't make me change my habits. I rarely took books home from school and didn't do homework very often. And yet, a single assignment stands out for me as if I did it yesterday. One evening my father helped me learn ten words I needed to know for a spelling test the next day. It happened more than six decades ago, but I still remember two words on that list and still know how to spell them today: *office* and *bicycle*.

Perhaps I remember them so clearly because it was the only time I recall either of my parents ever helping me with my schoolwork.

CHAPTER 3

Mermentau

I t's interesting that a place that's so hard to spell is a place so very dear in my memories. But from early childhood I always loved Mermentau, Louisiana. For me it was the heart of acceptance, encouragement, and pride.

Our family took many trips to Mermentau, deep in Cajun country, because both of my parents were raised there. My grandparents on my dad's side and my grandmother on my mother's side still lived in the small town of two hundred, located on the east bank of the Mermentau River west of Lafayette. When I was little, our whole family would visit. Then, when I turned twelve, Dad took me there to stay for the summer all by myself. I thought it was heaven. Although my brothers would visit for short periods, they never stayed for long, which meant I didn't have to compete with them for attention or put up with their bullying. Instead, for three months I could enjoy my grandparents all to myself and spend time in the fascinating place they called home.

Grandma and Grandpa lived literally a hundred yards from the swamp. The low-lying, spongy land was covered in water, shaded by cypress trees, and punctuated with water lilies. Spanish moss, floating in the humid breeze, warned, "Be careful, this is a swamp," but it also made for a beautiful, mysterious place. Alligators and snakes swam and basked in the sun not far from my grandparents' front door, and the birds made sounds that can only be heard in swampy woods and wetlands. At night, big bullfrogs joined the chorus. I can still remember lying in my bed in the dark, listening to the music they made, sounds that go straight to your soul in assurance of peace or in fear of pain.

There were no fans or air conditioning at my grandparents' house, so we slept with all the windows and doors open, hoping to catch a breeze as the damp night air moved slowly through the rooms and over our perspiring bodies. As I descended into sleep, I'd often hear a steam whistle pierce the thick night air, the long, lonesome sound of a train passing through on its way from Houston to New Orleans or back again. The whistle always had a high pitch when it was coming toward me and a low pitch when it was going away. By listening to the train's steam whistle, I could tell which way it was going. Finally the sound drifted into the night and disappeared, and I was able to close my eyes, breathe deeply, and fall asleep.

* * *

Life in Mermentau was the perfect combination of contentment and adventure. When I arrived, Grandma and Grandpa were always happy to see me. They gave me my own bedroom, something I'd never had at home, and asked me to help around the house, in their big garden, and out in the barn. I'd weed and water, feed the chickens and the pigs, keep the fire going when Grandma made lye soap, and help Grandpa butcher and smoke their meat.

I also spent a lot of time in the swamp by myself catching crawfish, fish, and turtles. I kept a fish box in the shallow water and filled it with live fish. If Grandma wanted to fix fish for supper, she'd say, "Glenn, what do you have in your fish box?" "I have two garfish and a nice catfish," I might reply. "Here's the dishpan," she'd say, handing it to me. "Bring me the garfish."

One of Grandma's specialties was garfish patties. After I skinned out my catch and cut their heads off, I'd take the fish to Grandma and she'd bone them, put the meat through the meat grinder, then add onions, spices, cracker crumbs, and eggs before frying the round patties in a skillet. I remember the taste like it was yesterday—a little greasy, but light and crispy. Delicious.

Other times, I would find a large land turtle and Grandma would make turtle stew. First, I'd cut the turtle's head off and hold it upside down to let the blood drain out. I would then use a hacksaw to separate the two sides of the shell so Grandma could get to the dark, tender meat.

If I'd found a turtle's nest, we'd have hard-boiled turtle eggs too, which looked and tasted a lot like chicken eggs, only smaller.

No matter what the meal, if there were guests for dinner that night—my aunts and uncles or family friends—Grandma was always sure to bring up the fact that I had caught what we were eating. Wasn't I a good fisherman and hunter? I felt so proud from her praise that I couldn't wait to go back to the swamp and catch some more. Her simple words made me feel needed and important, and I loved my newfound sense of self-confidence.

* * *

My grandparents didn't have refrigeration, so they relied on their smokehouse to cure and preserve their meat. The smokehouse was about seven by nine feet, with a six-foot-tall ceiling and a dirt floor. One small window provided light and let us see in. In the middle of the floor was a washtub, which held the fire that smoked the meat, and large crocks sat along the outer edges. In their smokehouse, Grandma and Grandpa cured hams, sausage, bacon, and boudin—a liver dressing packed inside sausage casing.

Curing was a two-step process. First, when we butchered we'd put some of the meat into the five-gallon crocks, then cover it with lard, brown sugar, and salt. It would stay there for one or two weeks before step number two: the actual smoking. At that point Grandpa would take the meat out, leaving it coated with fat and seasoning, and hang it from the rafters, where it would be smoked. Once the meat was hanging, it was a twenty-four-hour-a-day responsibility to make sure the fire never went out. Several times each night I'd hear Grandpa get up to check the smoke before I turned over and went back to sleep.

For the next few months, we'd have ham, bacon, and sausage to supplement the fish Grandpa and I caught, the chickens we slaughtered, and vegetables we harvested from the garden. Grandma would send me out to the smokehouse to get the meat she wanted for supper, which by that time had developed a thin coating of mold. She'd wipe it off, revealing the dark brown, very tender and delicious meat, and prepare a wonderful meal.

Grandma had other chores for me too. One was keeping our homemade mattresses soft and full. The Spanish moss that hung from the trees was our stuffing; we'd pull it down, dry it in the sun, and fill hand-sewn mattress covers with it. When they were freshly stuffed, the mattresses would be twelve to eighteen inches thick, but by the end of summer our bodies would have compressed them to only four or six inches. Grandma would enlist me to pull out the tamped-down moss, rinse it in water, and hang it on the fence to dry so our beds would again be fluffy and thick.

About once or twice a summer, Grandma would make lye soap in a large cast-iron kettle over a wood fire in the yard. My job was to keep the fire going under the pot while Grandma cooked the mixture of lard, water, and lye. It took several hours for the liquid to emulsify before Grandma poured it into molds where it would harden. The final product had a slight odor from the rendered fat, but it was good, pure soap.

We washed from a basin in the kitchen because in those years, my grandparents didn't have running water. When anyone wanted a drink, they used a metal dipper with a long wooden handle that hung near the back door by a large bucket filled with drinking water. Before indoor plumbing, every home had to have an outhouse, too. Ours was built by the state of Louisiana, and had good ventilation, a concrete floor, and two holes with lids.

One day I had a terrible scare in that outhouse. As I sat, minding my own business, I saw something that made my heart stop. There, dangling over the door, was one of the biggest snakes I'd ever seen, longer than the door was wide. Mind you, this was the same door I'd entered only minutes before and the one I'd hoped to exit through, too—soon! I don't remember how I got out of there as fast as I did, but I do remember killing that snake with one of Grandma's clothesline poles so I wouldn't find myself in that predicament again.

At night, when we didn't want to go all the way to the outhouse in the dark, especially when it was raining or cold, we used a chamber pot, a white porcelain enamel container with a lid. The lid was very noisy, so Grandma had crocheted a cover that fit over it to quiet the clinking sound. It was her job to rinse the chamber pots every morning, and mine to bring them back inside after they'd dried out in the sun.

I had little contact with my parents during those months, but one summer I needed more clothes and so I wrote a postcard to Mother. Grandma, sitting near me, noticed I had misspelled "clothes" and "Mermentau." Instead of criticizing, she carefully wrote out the two words on a separate piece of paper so I could copy them and learn the spelling. It was a small gesture of help, but one I've never forgotten.

By the end of my third summer at my grandparents' place, I was fourteen. Dad had come to get me the summers before, but that year I caught the bus in Mermentau and went to Houston, where I transferred to another bus that took me home to Baytown. I did this all by myself. It was a small accomplishment, but I was proud to be old enough to travel alone.

Mother and Dad were outside when I came into the yard—I'd walked the two and a half miles from the bus station to our house. "Hello!" I called to them as they came into view.

I was taller, brown from days spent outdoors, confident and happy. My voice had changed. Mother looked up, startled, and cried, "Oh my goodness, my little boy has grown up!"

I looked different and sounded different from when I'd left three months earlier. What my parents didn't know was that I was different on the inside too. Those summers were a very important time in my life. Grandma and Grandpa had offered me encouragement and surrounded me with love. They'd given me self-confidence and shaped me into a young man.

Now it was time for me to start thinking about high school. I had always had problems learning at school and I was still a poor reader and speller, but my summers in Mermentau had given me a new outlook on life. I was ready to see where it would take me.

CHAPTER 4

Cedar Bayou High

C edar Bayou High School was small, with only about twenty-five or thirty students in each grade. That made going to school there special. There were close bonds among the students, the parents, and the teachers that produced respect and valued friendships, many of which lasted a lifetime. You can be much more involved and accepting when you're one of thirty instead of one of hundreds. For my situation, going to a small high school meant I had lots of opportunities to succeed at the things I did best—but it also meant I had to be very careful to hide my poor reading.

In sports, I excelled. I played football for three years and loved it. My position was left tackle—though I could play both the offensive and the defensive—and my number was always 71. Because there were only twenty-nine students in my high school class, most of the boys were on the football team. There were no rules that you had to make good grades in order to stay on the team, so I was okay.

All the players had to memorize six pages of plays—but there was no reading. Like most playbooks, ours was a series of drawings, and I knew them all. Though I didn't recognize it at the time, I think in pictures rather than words, so anything explained with drawings or diagrams is easy for me to absorb and remember. I also think in three dimensions; for example when I look at a wall, I visualize the two-by-fours, the insulation, and the wiring. When I look at a lock, I see inside the lock and know how it works. And when I studied those playbook drawings, the X's, O's, and arrows became players on the field whose movements I could picture instantly, like I was watching a movie. It wasn't until many years later that I discovered most people don't see the world this way—and what an advantage it is that I do.

Our coaches were men of character, and they honed their players to believe in themselves and have a positive outlook on life. That was an especially valuable lesson for me, because when I was off the field and in the classroom I was operating in survival mode and just trying to get by.

There was never any consideration on my part to try to make A's and B's. I never made good grades and, as far as I saw it, chances were I never would. Rather than stressing out over grades like my friends did, I was under pressure to hide mine, and to keep anyone from knowing I was different. I made mostly C's, D's, and F's, which was about the best I thought I could do.

Still, I remained a happy kid with lots of friends who had lots of fun. I was good at sports and in shop, and I enjoyed my projects for Future Farmers of America. With all of my extracurricular and social activities, school was endurable—in fact, it was fun.

Part of that fun was girls—at least one girl in particular. We were juniors when I first saw Melva Maley in typing class. She was a beautiful, lively sixteen-year-old with wavy auburn hair and an infectious smile. I really wanted to get her attention. But being a bit of a class clown, I went about it the wrong way—and almost put myself out of the running before I even made it to the starting line.

Melva was standing at her typewriter reviewing some homework papers in Mrs. Schwietzer's typing class, and I decided it would be funny to move her chair back about four inches as I casually passed behind her desk. When she went to sit down she missed the chair completely and ended up on the floor, cute little skirt and all.

I didn't get a glimpse of her pretty smile after that stunt, believe me. For what seemed like the longest time afterward, she expressed little interest in me. In fact, she told a mutual friend that she thought I was silly, and I was afraid I'd lost any chance of ever being her boyfriend.

The small size of our class and her selection of available suitors turned out to be my big advantage. There were only four or five of us boys who didn't have girlfriends. Floyd didn't want one, and Dave was Melva's first cousin. Roy didn't take showers very often, and Bobby didn't play football. Taking all that into consideration, Melva chose me. It didn't hurt that I had wavy black hair, played football, and was the first guy at our high school to have a car.

We were a handsome pair. I was a football player, and she was the drum majorette. I took Melva to the local drive-in for a movie or to hamburger joints on Saturday nights, but many of our "dates" ended before they got started, with me and her dad, Guy, playing music at her house.

I played the mandolin and Guy played the fiddle. I could play music by ear—I've never been able to read music—and that worked out just fine. Often when I showed up at the

Maleys' house to pick up Melva for our date, Guy and I would sit down to play "just a song or two," and before we knew it, several hours had passed. Melva was never that thrilled to have her date commandeered, but I always enjoyed those evenings with her dad.

Making connections with other people, whether they were kids my age or adults, was something I excelled at—it was part of the way I survived and hid my poor reading and writing abilities. For example, every fall I would take off from school on Thursdays to go duck hunting, *with* the principal's permission.

My family lived in the woods on a bayou, and it didn't take me long to figure out that the best day to hunt ducks was Thursday. The ducks were just starting to settle down from the previous weekend's hunt, and they hadn't yet heard the first shots on Saturday morning that would unsettle them again.

On Friday mornings, I would go to the principal's office to get an excuse for being absent from school the day before. When the principal asked where I'd been, I told him the truth. He liked my honest approach, and wrote on the excuse sheet, "Glenn was hunting duck." He didn't seem to think this was a big deal either—after all, duck hunting season only lasted six weeks, and I was being truthful.

Coach Adams also knew I was an upstanding, good kid and gave me a little bit of leverage. One day several of us boys slipped out of school, got in my car, and went to the pool hall, which just so happened to be across the street from the police station. Little did we know that Coach Adams, who was also the driver's education teacher, was bringing his class to the police station that day so they could take their driver's license tests.

During our game I stepped outside of the pool hall, cue in hand, to watch the traffic go by. When I looked across the street, there was Coach Adams, watching me. We exchanged a little wave, and I went back inside.

The next day at school, Coach Adams explained to the football team the advantages of not skipping school and the disadvantages of going to a pool hall—especially one located just across the street from a police station.

* * *

But not everyone was as willing to overlook my shenanigans and see my charms.

By high school, I had taken on the role of being a clown, putting on a show and trying to be funny. I continued to be polite to all the teachers and respectful of their authority, but I also covered up the lack of self-esteem brought on by my reading problems by making the other kids laugh. It worked: Even Melva wasn't aware of my big secret for the longest time. I goofed off to distract my friends because I was scared that everyone would find out how hard it was for me to do something as simple for them as reading. Sure, I could struggle through a short assignment or a newspaper article, but I would never be able to read a book or write an essay like the rest of the students could.

English was naturally my least favorite subject. My English teachers generally looked past my inability to keep up with the assignments, but senior year I got called on the carpet for what was perceived to be lazy behavior.

Mrs. Boyd, our English teacher, had given us a writing assignment that was due on a Friday. I didn't turn anything in, and I really didn't give it much thought since that was how I often dealt with these insurmountable tasks. At lunchtime the next Monday, Mrs. Boyd called me to her room.

"Have you turned in your paper that was due Friday?" she asked, knowing the answer.

"No, ma'am," I replied.

"Have you started it?" she asked.

"No, ma'am," I repeated.

"Well, we are just not going to have that!" she exclaimed. "That paper was due on Friday, and here it is Monday. Everyone else in the class turned in their papers except you. If you don't turn in that paper by tomorrow, I'm going to give everyone in the class an F because you didn't do your work."

My only answer, which I delivered respectfully, was that it was okay to give me an F for not doing the work, but it wouldn't be right to punish everyone else for something I didn't do. And I never did turn in the paper—I simply couldn't complete the assignment. Fortunately, everyone was graded fairly, including me. I got an F.

The next time I walked into English class, I politely greeted the teacher with "Good morning" and took my seat. I pretended like nothing had happened, but inside I was ashamed. We never discussed the situation again.

Just like in elementary school, my friends were still trying to cover for me and help me muddle through. One semester,

I took a journalism class to meet my English requirements. It was taught by Mr. Watkins, the basketball coach, and I was assigned to write about sports. Our articles appeared in the school newspaper. We worked in groups, so two of my classmates had the same assignment as me. They ended up writing all the articles, even though we got the same credit. So there was my name in the sports section of the Cedar Bayou High paper with the byline "sports reporter"!

It wouldn't surprise me if those long-ago classmates knew I was a poor reader who had trouble writing. They probably didn't want me to know they knew, so they just took care of me. Helping one another, whether it was constructive or a cover-up, was what our close-knit high school class did.

There were some classes I enjoyed and did okay in, however. I liked science and math because I understood what the teachers were talking about. I could visualize the concepts in pictures, and sometimes I knew what the teacher was describing before the words were out of his mouth. But my talents in science and math could never fully shine for one simple reason: we were tested with written exams. If I had been given more time, or if I'd been allowed to solve problems or draw diagrams instead of writing out my answers, I could have done much better. But that was never a consideration.

* * *

As the end of my senior year approached, the concerns of a young man about to enter the world as an adult occupied my mind more and more. My first worry was whether I'd be able to graduate come June. I knew I had finals ahead of me, and I wasn't convinced I could pass them. About eight weeks before the end of school they posted our three-year high school averages on a bulletin board outside the school library for everyone to see, and my ranking was not a good sign of things to come. The names were arranged with the highest averages at the top and the lowest at the bottom. It didn't take long for me to find myself at the end of the list. There, second to last, was "Glenn Harrington" with an embarrassing "72" beside it.

Although everyone had seen the list, no one said a word to me about my dismal grades. But I sure started to worry about them and what they meant for my future. Would I be able to finish high school with a diploma, like everybody else? If I did, how would I make a living after graduation without a skill? I was very handy at fixing cars and figuring out how things worked, but I didn't have my sights set on being an auto mechanic or a refinery worker like my dad. College was out of the question; I simply wasn't college material. There was always the military—it was 1951, the Korean War was on, and I had a draft card marked 1-A, which meant that like it or not, they would probably be contacting me once school was out. Whatever was about to happen, it would be a big change. But for now, all I could see were doors closing behind me and none opening in their place.

Then something miraculous was delivered to me, in a surprising package. One day I was glancing through the paper and spotted a small article, about two inches long, a length I could read without too much trouble. Its headline caught my eye because it was about volunteering for the military. I had already resigned myself to the fact that I would be drafted, which meant four years of regular service plus four years as a reservist. The article said that any young man voluntarily joining the military before April 30, 1951, would serve the regular four years but could forgo the additional four years in the reserves. It seemed like a gift.

I took the article to the superintendent of schools, explained my situation to him, and told him that I needed to enlist before April 30—which was only a week or so away. Lo and behold, he agreed, and added that if I volunteered for the Air Force I wouldn't have to take finals and would still receive a diploma. Well, this proposal was a godsend. I would graduate, I didn't have to take finals, and the draft was no longer an issue. I would also have a job for the next four years in the newly designated U.S. Air Force, now its own branch of the military separate from the Army, where I was sure I could gain some useful skills. So on April 27, three days before the deadline and six weeks before graduation, I joined up. I didn't know then what a turning point in my life it would be.

* * *

One other decision had been weighing heavily on me too—how to ask Melva to marry me. We'd been going steady for about a year, and I knew this was the girl I wanted to spend the rest of my life with. We'd talked about our future together, but with so many other decisions up in the air I'd been hesitant. Now it was time to ask for Guy's permission and see about getting engaged.

Guy and I had been doing a lot of things together, like going duck hunting in the marsh and fishing off the south end of Galveston Island. We had established a close relationship. When I showed up at the Maleys' house looking a little nervous, I don't think there was much doubt in his mind about why I was there.

After a few questions regarding my plans after high school and a comment or two about Melva's mother, Guy gave me permission to marry his daughter. I think he had the normal reservations of any father, but he knew how much I loved Melva and that I would provide for her in every way I could.

With his blessing, the next step was to come up with the money I needed to buy an engagement ring. At the time, my after-school job was cleaning a doctor's office for $9 a week. That wouldn't get me far, so I had to formulate another plan. My good friend Hoop came to the rescue with an interesting series of exchanges that would put a ring in my pocket.

Hoop's brother, Bubba, had an engagement ring and wedding band set that he'd bought for his girlfriend. The only problem was, they'd broken up and she'd returned the rings—bad for him but good for me. I had a 1929 Oakland coupe that I'd bought for $25 two years before but didn't need, and Hoop wanted it. So I gave Hoop the car, Hoop gave Bubba the $25, and Bubba gave me the rings.

On our next date, I picked Melva up to take her to the movies in my 1941 two-door Plymouth. Little did she know that I had an engagement ring hidden under the front seat. When we got back to her house after our date, I pulled out the ring and asked her to marry me.

I was relieved and thrilled when she said yes. With my new appointment in the U.S. Air Force I knew I'd be able to support my soon-to-be wife. We could get married as soon as I found out where I'd be stationed. Astonishingly, my series of problems had untangled, and my future was looking brighter than I'd ever imagined.

Before I knew it, it was time to head off for boot camp. Mother, Dad, Melva, and I drove to the recruiting station in Houston, where I'd be processed and shipped off for military training. When we got to the station, Dad double-parked in front for a quick good-bye. I got out of the car, grabbed my bag, gave Melva a peck on the cheek, and walked in with hardly a glance over my shoulder.

My life as a newly minted Air Force recruit had begun.

CHAPTER 5

Air Force Instructor

That afternoon I was sworn into the U.S. Air Force.

My life was no longer my own—it now belonged to the U.S. Air Force. And so did my thick, wavy black hair. The first stop once we arrived at Lackland Air Force Base in San Antonio the next morning was the barbershop, where our hair was cut to an eighth-inch stubble. After the haircuts they marched us to the supply room, and we were told we could keep one set of civilian clothes. Everything else would be shipped home.

We took off everything but our undershorts, set aside a pair of shoes, a shirt, and pants, and lined up to receive our uniforms. Each recruit was given fatigues, a pair of work boots called brogans, pants, shirts, a coat, a hat and cap, undershorts, socks, and long underwear with a trap door. We were also issued a heavy canvas duffle bag, about two feet by four feet with a lock on top and a carrying strap, to hold all our new belongings.

Already, we were transformed: nearly bald and naked, with nothing to call our own but what the U.S. government had issued us. It was a psychological exercise to literally strip us down so we could be figuratively stripped down too— and then do whatever the Air Force ordered us to, without question.

The shower that came next let us know who was in charge in case there was any residual doubt. As we washed, a drill sergeant watched to make sure we didn't miss anything. Then they dusted us down with what I'm sure was DDT to kill any head or body lice we might have. Finally, we were allowed to put on our new undershorts so we could be given a complete medical exam—from teeth to toenails, and everything in between.

* * *

I knew enough to expect all of this, but the next part, seeing my new living quarters, was a bit of a surprise. Instead of the barracks I'd pictured, we were marched to long rows of canvas tents, each with dirt floors and enough cots and footlockers to house eight men. Lackland had been built to handle 20,000 soldiers, but that spring of 1951, at the height of the Korean War, more than 80,000 recruits poured into the base and "Tent City" grew up on its grounds to accommodate us all.

Four days before, I had been a student at Cedar Bayou High School. Now I was sharing a tent with seven other guys, shaving at rows of lavatories set up outside for washing, and sharing a communal outhouse and community shower with hundreds of other young soldiers. It was a new world, a place I was about to grow up in—and in a hurry.

In the following days, we learned how to stand at attention, how to bark, "Yes, sir!" and "No, sir!" and of course, we learned how to march.

Though I had always been obsessed with cars and was proud of the '41 Plymouth roadster I'd lovingly restored in high school, marching became my new form of transportation. We marched everywhere: up and down the streets, around the parade grounds, to and from chow hall, in rain and hot sun, for hours and hours. If we had nothing else to do, we always had marching. The strange thing was, we never seemed to get anywhere.

* * *

After we'd spent about a week in our crowded quarters in Tent City, the higher-ups at Lackland decided to ship some of the airmen to Sheppard Air Force Base in Wichita Falls, Texas, to ease the crowding and make way for new recruits. I was one of the recruits bussed three hundred miles to the new base for my six weeks of basic training.

Training went by quickly and without much trouble—until the last week. At the end of basic, we all had to take written aptitude tests to see where we would be assigned and what type of work we'd be doing for the next four years. All of a sudden, those same fears from high school came rushing back. Would I be able to pass the tests? Would the grades be posted for everyone to see? On the morning of the exams, I could feel my throat tightening and my breath quickening. I was scared.

Officers led groups of twenty-five recruits to a series of classrooms. Sweat was gathering on my brow. But as soon as I saw the booklets and heard the instructions, my fears began to ease up. Each booklet was only six to eight pages, with mostly true or false, multiple choice, or fill-in-the-blank questions, and we could take as long as we needed to complete each exam. Some had math problems or drawings, but very few required writing.

When we finished our tests, the sergeant sitting at the front of the room graded each one, wrote our scores on the cover, handed the booklets back to us, and then sent us to another room where someone would look over each airman's scores and talk to him about what he wanted to do in the Air Force.

My score on the clerical section was a zero, which was no surprise. But I did very well on the mechanical test, in fact had made a 5 out of 5. The man behind the desk asked me, "Would you like to be an aircraft mechanic?" Well, that was exactly what I wanted to do, so I said yes. And that's how I ended up at the Sheppard AFB Aircraft & Engine School for the next five months.

* * *

Sometimes life takes turns that you never could have foreseen, leading you in directions that change your life forever. Meeting Melva veered my life down a path that I never expected, one that brings me joy every day we're together. Reading a short newspaper article led to me join the Air Force, another fortuitous moment that sent my life in a whole new direction. If I hadn't looked at the *Houston Chronicle* on that spring day in 1951, I might never have become a teacher.

Once we finished our aircraft mechanic training at the Aircraft & Engine School, six young men were chosen to stay on as instructors. I was one of them.

I was proud and concerned at the same time. I had made good grades during my training, or I would never have been chosen to teach other recruits how to repair aircraft engines. No one had ever asked how well I could read, since so much of what we learned came from watching, listening, and doing. But wouldn't teaching require me to read? I'd have to wait and see. The orders were out and the choice was made: I was assigned to be an A & E School instructor.

All of the other instructors were also graduates of the school, like me. We would teach what we'd just learned, plus any new material presented at workshops throughout the year. The master sergeant in charge of the school provided us with outlines for our classes, and to make sure we were teaching the material as we should, a tech sergeant would visit our classrooms and evaluate our performance.

I knew I was going to have to find ways to instruct my students that didn't require reading and writing in front of them. I'd have to teach them in the same way I learned: with diagrams, through observation, and by visualizing in three dimensions how the parts of an engine worked together. They'd need to stop thinking in words and start thinking in pictures. In other words, they'd need to think and learn just like me.

* * *

By the time I graduated from Sheppard's A & E School and received my assignment to stay on as an instructor, it was near the first of December. The war in Korea was in full swing, and a rumor was making its way around the base that no one would be allowed to go home on Christmas leave. I was crushed. Melva and I had planned to get married as soon as I found out where I'd be stationed, and Christmas would have been the perfect time for a wedding in Cedar Bayou.

All through basic training and my time at A & E School, Melva had been writing to me, just about every day. I was able to read her letters, but I didn't write back very often. Most of my writing wasn't legible. As is often the case with dyslexics, I also have dysgraphia, which means not only do I have trouble organizing thoughts on paper, my handwriting is also very poor. Oftentimes I cannot read my own long-hand. It wasn't until later that I learned printing was much easier for me and more legible, and I started to print instead of write in cursive.

But the first of December I wrote a short letter to Melva letting her know our marriage plans would have to be put on hold. Then, about a week later, out of the blue came orders that we were going to have a two-week leave for Christmas after all! I called Melva and told her, "Honey, if we're going to do this, we need to do it now."

In a whirlwind, Melva made all the plans, invited the guests, and was ready and waiting when I arrived home just before Christmas. We got married in the Methodist church in Cedar Bayou, the largest church in our hometown and the place most people got married. A preacher friend of my father's performed the ceremony, and many of my relatives, including my grandmother from Mermentau, Uncle Bradley, and Uncle Skeet, came to the wedding. Hoop, by then also in the Air Force, was my best man.

On that day, December 22, 1951, Melva and I began our new life together, our two lives coming together as one.

* * *

Those two weeks of leave flew by faster than the blink of an eye. After the wedding, my new bride and I traveled to Mexico for a quick honeymoon, then to New Orleans for a family funeral before heading home. Before I knew it we were back at Sheppard Air Force Base and I was standing before a class of A & E School students with a vast blackboard staring out behind me.

You may wonder how someone who was a poor reader, who had always disliked the classroom and dreaded taking tests and writing papers, could become a good instructor in the United States Air Force. At first, I wondered that too. Then I put on my thinking cap and found ways to get around reading and writing in front of others, and instead found ways to connect with them—just like I'd always done.

My spelling was so bad that I couldn't write on the blackboard in my classrooms. So I took to drawing detailed pictures of the engines I was teaching my students to repair, with cross sections of carburetors, crankshafts, and cylinders. I would sometimes go to class early so I had time to illustrate my diagrams carefully, in great detail, before the students arrived. It worked. Soon the young airmen in my classes were visualizing these complex engines just as I did. Seeing diagrams rather than words was just as important to them as it was to me.

Sometimes, I would come back to the same classroom several days after I had taught a lesson to find that my drawings were still on the blackboard. Other instructors were using them to teach their classes too! That made me smile, because I enjoyed teaching and knew I was turning out to be a good instructor—and I was also working hard to keep the other instructors and supervisors from knowing my big secret.

In the beginning, all my drawings were in black and white. Then, later in 1952, I decided to go high-tech by using colored chalk I bought off-base. One day the tech sergeant who was visiting my class said, "Hey, where'd you get that colored chalk?" I told him where I'd found it in town, and the next day, there was colored chalk on the ledge of every blackboard in the school.

Again, I smiled. My high school hobby of tinkering with engines and fixing cars was starting to pay off.

* * *

One of the engines that was not in our curriculum that year was the R-4360. Six of these engines, plus four jet engines, powered the B-36 bomber, making it the largest bomber ever commissioned in the United States Air Force at that time.

Sheppard AFB soon saw the need to add instruction on the R-4360 to our curriculum. The only way to learn about the engine was at the Pratt and Whitney School in Hartford, Connecticut, which was also the factory where this engine was made.

Out of seventy-five A & E School instructors, two were picked to go. I was one of them. The choice shocked me. I knew I was a good teacher, but I'd never been sure how good a job I'd done covering up my poor reading around the other instructors. Now I knew. I was honored to be chosen.

Another staff sergeant and I would be sent to Hartford for two weeks to learn all we could about this powerful engine, then bring the information back to Sheppard so we could teach the other instructors and add it to the school's curriculum. But first we had to get security clearance. Pratt and Whitney had a large research and development department, and the machinery we were about to see there had implications not only for the Korean War, but for future military engagements as well.

After arriving at the school, right off the bat a high-ranking officer came into our classroom and told us that anything we saw in R&D was not to leave the building. We could not tell our families, our girlfriends, not even fellow military personnel. Further, the Air Force could test us to see whether we would talk about it. It was a sobering speech.

Next, eight men in orange jumpsuits arrived. They were our security escort. They took us from our first-floor classrooms up to the second floor, and we spent several hours walking wide aisles among the various projects, including an atomic engine that was being developed for use in aircraft. Though it worked, the engine posed a major challenge: its weight was too great to allow it to fit into a plane. Eventually, Pratt and Whitney would use the technology to power the first atomic submarine.

But we weren't there to study the new atomic engine. We were there to learn all we could about the R-4360. Most of the instruction revolved around studying cutaways of the engine, then working hands-on to take apart and put together the machinery ourselves. It was right up my alley. Though we did have manuals and handouts with model drawings, we were allowed to spend time with them out of the classroom and back at Sheppard. Eagerly, I grabbed all the materials I could get my hands on so I could study them closely and share them with my students.

By the time I finished at the Pratt and Whitney School I understood the R-4360 and its propeller well enough to teach them back in Wichita Falls. After about six months, we added instruction on the engine to our program, using similar cutaways and samples of all the major parts. My memory and visual thinking style made me an excellent choice to carry this information back to our school.

* * *

The goal of any aircraft mechanic is to become a crew chief. But for the first two years I taught at Sheppard, there was no certification program for our mechanics to learn what a crew chief does. The Air Force remedied that in 1953, adding a five-day course titled Duties and Responsibilities of a Crew Chief. Eight instructors were selected to teach the course, and once again I made the cut.

To teach how to be a crew chief, first you have to become certified to be one yourself. So the eight of us did, using B-25s as the planes whose maintenance we would oversee. The primary duty of a crew chief is inspections—daily, weekly, monthly, and according to the number of takeoffs, landings, hours of flight, and so on. So in our shack was a big wall of clipboards where we recorded our inspections and where we approved and signed off on our mechanics' work. It turned out to be a very successful program at the school, and I was glad to be a part of it.

* * *

Then in 1953, not long after I began teaching our new crew chief certification program, the unexpected happened. I received orders to go to Japan and take part in the war.

My assignment was to join a maintenance group that would service B-26s fighting in Korea. I would be using my mechanical skills firsthand for the first time in my military career. Rather than instructing other mechanics heading to the front, I would be one of them.

I got all my shots and prepared to leave. I was ready to do my part. There was just one thing holding me back, and it was a big one: Melva was pregnant with our first child.

Together, we made arrangements so she could move back to Baytown to be near our folks when the baby arrived. I hated the thought of leaving her halfway across the world, but I had no choice. Everything was set for me to go.

Or so we thought. One morning not long before I was scheduled to leave, I arrived at the school to find I had orders posted on the bulletin board. I was to report to the commanding officer at 10:00 a.m. There was no indication as to why.

I entered his office right on time and came to attention with a brisk salute.

"Sergeant Glenn L. Harrington, AF18402078, reporting as requested, sir!"

The commanding officer looked up from his desk and returned my salute. Looking me in the eye, he asked in a deep voice, "Sergeant, is your wife pregnant?"

"Yes, sir!" I barked back proudly.

He looked back down at his desk. "Sergeant, we don't send airmen overseas whose wives are pregnant," the CO informed me. "We'll cut you new orders and catch you later. Dismissed."

And in the flash of an eye, my future had changed again. I didn't have to take part in Korea. I'd be home for the birth of my daughter. And by the time "later" came around, the war would be over—I'd never have to serve overseas.

Instead, my next big adventure was about to begin.

Chapter 6

My Learning Program

Our beautiful baby, Beth Marie Harrington, was born July 6, 1953, in the Sheppard AFB hospital. I couldn't have been more proud. Life was about to change dramatically for me—in more ways than one.

Though I'd just started my new job as a father, my role as an Air Force instructor was winding down. As much as I'd loved teaching, and as gifted as I seemed to be at it, the fact that the Air Force was phasing out gasoline engines in favor of jet engines caused me to be reassigned. Had I chosen to reenlist at the end of my four-year stint, the government would have sent me to jet engine mechanic school and I would have continued teaching. As it was, I chose not to re-up, and instead spent the rest of my enlistment running a refueling shack on the base.

There was an upside to my career change. My shift was from 4 p.m. to midnight every evening, hours that permitted me to spend the day at home with my wife and new daughter. In addition, two civilians, college students, worked alongside me, which made an otherwise boring job more interesting. They liked the late shift because it allowed them to go to school during the day and work at night, and when things were slow at the station, they could study. The boys would bring their books, spread them out on the desk, and burn the midnight oil in between pumping gas and accepting fuel shipments.

It wasn't long before I became interested in their subject, geology. I started asking them questions, then reviewing the diagrams and illustrations in their books. To my surprise, I understood everything they were studying.

Like most people, the young men I worked with never suspected I was a poor reader—but they did know I had a sharp mind and a curious nature. Pretty soon, they were encouraging me to go to college. To them it was no big deal—why shouldn't I? But for me, the idea of college was revolutionary.

When I'd left high school, the last thing I ever considered doing was going back to school, for any reason. In my mind, poor readers didn't survive college—they barely survived high school. But now, with several years of successful teaching behind me, I allowed myself to open that door a crack and peek in. I knew I could teach. I knew I could learn. Maybe there was a way. I'd loved being an instructor at the A & E School. College might offer me a way to make a living doing something I enjoyed—teaching.

I also had to think about my future and my family. In a few months, my four years in the Air Force would be up and I would be discharged. I still didn't really have a skill for making a living. Sure, I knew the mechanics of a gasoline-powered aircraft engine, had taught airmen how to take apart and fix them, and could run a refueling shack, but where would that get me in the civilian world? Not far. Melva and I could move back to Baytown and I could try to get a job at one of the refineries. But that wasn't the life I wanted. Having had a taste of something I felt I was born to do, I wanted more. I wanted to study science and to teach.

Melva and I talked about it, and she was behind me 100 percent. We looked into the GI Bill and found out it would pay me $160 a month to go to college. That seemed like an extraordinary amount of money—our hospital bill for having Beth had only been $5.40, after all. The more I thought about it, the more I convinced myself that maybe, just maybe, I could pull this off.

On June 1, 1954, I took the big leap. That was the day I enrolled in Midwestern University in Wichita Falls, ten months before my stint with the U.S. Air Force was over.

* * *

Looking back, starting my college career while I was still in the military was the perfect situation. During the day I went to my two summer school classes, American History before 1865 and English 101. Afternoons and evenings I worked at the refueling shack and could study when things got slow, just like my employees did. When I wasn't at school or at work, I was helping out Melva or hitting the books. It was a lot to juggle, but by starting college while I was still in the military I was able to test the waters, see if I had what it took to go to college while still earning an airman's income to support my family.

Those first few days, I wasn't so sure Midwestern was the place for me. The morning I registered for classes, it was pouring down rain. By the time I found a parking space, located the right building, and joined the end of a long line, it seemed like the fates were trying to tell me something. "You're not college material," they whispered in my ear. I shook it off and stepped up to register for my first freshman credits.

Classes began, and my doubts continued. My history professor was a tall Republican from East Texas who laid down the law on day one as to what he would or would not tolerate in his class—even down to the type of pen we were allowed to write with.

Ballpoint pens were the latest thing, but Professor Smith wanted no part of them. Before ballpoints, everyone used fountain pens, which had to be filled with ink and were very messy. But nothing compared to the mess a leaky ballpoint left behind—big black circles of ink ruining shirt pockets and staining desk tops.

The professor had two rules: there would be lots of note-taking in his class, but pity the fool who showed up with a ballpoint in a pocket or purse. We all agreed it would be better to write with our own blood than go against this edict.

In English, I faced a different kind of challenge, but a familiar one. The assignment the first day was to write a short paper. "One page before the bell" was ringing in my ears as I opened my notebook and tightly gripped my pen. But I did what I could and turned in my paper along with everyone else.

The next day, my English professor went over some of the papers the other students had written, but not mine. Toward the end of class he called me up to his desk where no one could see or hear us and showed me a few things about my writing that needed work.

First he pointed to the page where I had written "ov." "Now Mr. Harrington, I think what you meant here was 'of,'" he kindly said. "Down here you have 'haft,'" he continued. "I think what you meant was 'have to.' 'Haft' isn't really a word." It was the first time someone had spoken to me discreetly and kindly about my deficiencies when it came to writing. I was grateful that he didn't embarrass me.

* * *

It was in those first weeks of college that I, at the age of twenty-one, decided that I needed to develop my own learning program if I was going to survive.

Less self-conscious now that I was a married man and father with three years of teaching behind me, I began with a technique I privately referred to as "power listening." First off, I always sat in the second row, where I could be close to the teacher and to the blackboard. Second, I kept my eyes fixed on the professor's face at all times. When I did this, I heard every word he said. The moment I let my eyes drift away, I'd begin to miss words and details. Eye contact was crucial.

The next part of my learning program relied on note-taking. My motto was "Never stop writing!" If I couldn't keep up with the professor's lecture, I'd sketch, draw diagrams, or copy whatever he'd put on the blackboard. I numbered and organized my notes when the class was over, and usually I'd have from four to ten pages of information.

Because of my difficulty reading books, these notes became my lifeline. Once I got the words and pictures down on paper, the learning process had begun.

Next, the review process kicked in. I would go home, rewrite the notes, then rewrite them again. By the time I'd been over the material three times, it would be reduced to the most important points—one or two pages. Before a test, I'd copy these points onto three-by-five cards and keep them in my shirt pocket to review when I was on a coffee break at the fueling shack or waiting in the car while Melva ran errands. After I'd read the material eight or ten times, I was ready to be tested.

I soon discovered through my learning program that professors taught in many different ways. Some explained everything in detail, and others relied on students to learn the bulk of the material from their books. I was not going to get far if I had to count on reading, so when I encountered a professor who didn't explain everything, I asked lots of questions in class, then showed up at his door for office hours. Typically, the professors welcomed this because they saw I was engaged and listening, and because my questions created a dialogue that the whole class could be a part of.

* * *

At the end of first summer session, using my system of listening, taking notes, and asking questions, I made a passable grade in Professor Smith's American History class. In English 101, I got an F.

Two days later, when time came to register for the second summer session, I swallowed my pride and signed up for English 101 again.

Making an F is not a failure. Refusing to go back and try to do better is. The second time I took English 101, I made a D. My pattern for taking English courses in college was set.

I have jokingly told people that I had four years of undergraduate-level English, but they only gave me two years' credit. I knew all the professors in that department because I was in most of their classes more than once. The second time I took the course, most would give me a passing grade.

It wasn't easy. Once, I walked into a class I was taking for the second time and the teacher turned and greeted me with, "Good morning, Glenn." Then she turned to the class and said, "Folks, this is Glenn. He is one of our mascots in the English Department."

What I needed to finish my English requirement was support, not discouragement. I hid my hurt and forged ahead.

I didn't give up and finished all of my undergraduate English requirements. In one case, I even made a B—because I knew about pride and what it meant to keep a secret.

I had a friend who worked nights in a liquor store, and sometimes I would keep him company. The two of us would study in the back room when things got slow out front.

One night we were in the back studying and someone came in, so my friend went out to the counter to wait on the customer. He came back a minute later and asked, "Don't you have a Miss Lee for English?"

I did, and I was somewhat shocked to discover what my friend told me next: This quiet literature professor came in every Thursday to pick up a case of vodka.

Knowing I was polite—and that I could use every bit of help I could get in English—my friend asked me if I'd like to take the case out to her car. In a flash I jumped up, grabbed the box from the shelf, and carried it out front. "Hello, Miss Lee," I greeted her. "Would you like me to put this in your car?"

She looked surprised and a little uncomfortable to see me, but she agreed. Every Thursday for the next few weeks, when Professor Lee came in I was there to greet her, retrieve her case of vodka, and carry it to her car.

By the end of the semester, I had the best grade I would ever receive in an English class: I'd been rewarded with a B for my good manners and my discretion.

* * *

The challenges I faced in college went beyond the difficulties I had navigating the English curriculum. Money was another concern that was never far from my mind.

In the 1950s, there were no student loans; it was pay as you go. I arranged to pay for my classes at the end of each semester before registering for the new term, but worrying about tuition, our house payment, groceries, and bills sometimes kept me up nights.

In order to receive the full $160 I got every month as part of the GI Bill, I had to carry fifteen credit hours each semester. I also had to work at least forty hours a week to take care of my wife and children. By January of 1955, during my sophomore year at Midwestern, we had grown our family to include a second daughter, Marsha Kay. Melva did a great job scrimping and saving to support my goal of earning a college degree and making a better life for our family: we ate a lot of Spam, beans and cornbread, and hamburger meat in those years. Melva sewed all the girls' clothing and her own, and she never complained about driving an older car— she knew I'd make sure our vehicles were well maintained and dependable. Although I sometimes doubted that I could pull off getting a college degree, Melva never did. She supported me and believed in me, no matter what.

My jobs in those years weren't particularly glamorous, but they put food on the table. In the first year after I was discharged from the Air Force, I worked at a service station before I became a night dispatcher for the Lane Wells Oil Field Maintenance Company. Then I took a job as an assistant to a man scouting for locations to drill oil wells—I just couldn't seem to wash my hands of oil. I did fieldwork and drew maps for his reports while he looked for oil companies to buy his claims. It was the perfect job for a poor reader with superior spatial skills: plotting and drawing but very little reading. Unfortunately, the job ended rather abruptly one day when my boss came into the office acting strange. That night he was put in a mental institution, and I never saw him again.

It was a particularly rough turn of events for our family because my boss was committed a month before Christmas, and once I closed up the office for his wife, I was out of a job.

Unemployment checks didn't exist then, and I had two baby girls looking forward to a visit from Santa, so I needed to find a job—fast.

I must have visited every business in Wichita Falls the next day, going door to door, up and down both sides of Main Street, inquiring about job openings at each and every clothing store, bank, restaurant, and five-and-dime. I was almost back to my car when I swung open the door to Sears and Roebuck.

I knew Sears had probably already hired all their Christmas help, and an inquiry to the manager confirmed it. But as I turned, dejected, to leave, she said, "Wait. We do have one thing available. We haven't hired our Santa Claus yet." I stopped, did an about-face, and in a deep voice exclaimed, "Ho, ho, ho!" I'd found my job.

There was one little girl from that December of 1957 I'll never forget. Her mother came to see me one Friday afternoon, asking for my help. The child, who had always loved Santa, was starting to ask questions, and her mother wanted her to believe for one more year. Could she enlist me to keep the Christmas spirit going? Of course, I said yes.

By the time the little girl was in line the next day, I had memorized all the details her mother had shared: the girl's Christmas gift from the year before, the name of her little brother, and her teacher's name at school.

The young mother winked at me as they reached my gilded chair. "Hello, Susie," I called, and the five-year-old glanced up at me in surprise. "Would you like to sit in my lap?"

By the time I'd asked her if she liked the little pink doll I'd given her the year before, Susie's eyes were locked on mine. "How's your brother Timmy?" I inquired. "Are you doing well in Mrs. Silver's class?"

It was obvious that she was sitting in the lap of the real, the one and only Santa Claus.

As she told me what she wanted for Christmas her mother leaned in and nodded. Our eyes met, and I knew this smiling, proud parent would enjoy one more magical Christmas with her innocent little girl.

* * *

At Midwestern, I had declared geology as my major. Just as I'd experienced during my nights at the refueling shack poring over my young employees' books, science clicked for me. I often understood theories before the professor had finished explaining them; it was as though I could see the science in my mind. Whether it was chemistry, physics, geology, or thermodynamics, the faculty saw I had an aptitude for scientific concepts, and soon I was working as a lab assistant in a variety of classes.

One man in particular had a great impact on me: Mr. Ryan. He taught geology and hired me as his lab assistant. As head of the geology department, he arranged for me to work nights as a janitor in the building and as the bus mechanic and driver for the geology department bus.

He was also the only person in this world other than Melva who noticed and was concerned about my reading and wanted to help. No one else, not even my own parents, had done that for me.

It happened very quietly and respectfully. I was walking by his office one day and he called me in. "You have a problem with reading, don't you?" he asked. "Well yes sir, I do," I replied. I'd never been asked that question before.

In his deep, kind voice he said, "I have a friend over in the Ferguson Building who is signing up students for a remedial reading class. I'm headed over there right now. Would you like me to introduce you?"

I don't know if he really knew the gentleman or not, but we walked over there together and I met Mr. Ryan's "friend." I signed up for the class and picked up my books. But even with that encouragement, my lack of self-esteem about my reading wouldn't allow me to continue. I realized the very first night that I couldn't even read the remedial material, so I never went back.

And yet, Mr. Ryan wouldn't let me fail.

One thing he did in particular bonded us forever. Though I was supposed to pay for my college tuition at the end of each semester, I had let several of these notes expire without taking care of them. The university continued to allow me to register for classes, and so I let it ride, knowing I would sell our house after I earned my degree, make good on the notes, and square myself with the university. Then, six months before graduation when I went to sign up for my final-semester courses, I was stopped by the finance officer and told I could no longer be a student until I paid off my outstanding tuition.

As much as I tried to reason with the man and insist I was good for the money, he wouldn't listen. I left in a panic. I knew there was no way to borrow that kind of cash, that selling our house before graduation would leave us with a whole new set of problems, and that I couldn't ask my family to cover my schooling. After a long talk that night with Melva, we decided reluctantly that my hopes for a college degree were through. Grades weren't about to defeat me— my grades were fine. Money would end my college dreams, pure and simple.

After considering every option and seeing all of them come to a dead end, Melva and I decided our only alternative was to head back to Baytown, where I would find a job in a refinery.

I went over to Mr. Ryan's house the next day to tell him I wouldn't be returning in the summer for my last semester. I knew he'd want to know. But instead of simply wishing me well, Mr. Ryan said, "That doesn't sound right. There must be some mistake. Let me go over to the university and talk to them. We'll figure this out. You go home, and don't do anything until I get in touch with you."

About an hour later he showed up at the house and said there was no problem. "Go back and register," he told me. "They'll give you a note for your last semester." I believed him, and he was right. And so I finished my final coursework at Midwestern.

As college wound down, Melva and I put our house on the market in anticipation of our move once graduation was over. About a week before commencement, we sold the house and I went down to the university to pay off my tuition. That's when I discovered that Mr. Ryan had cosigned all the papers, telling the finance officer if I didn't pay the notes, he would.

I have often told people Mr. Ryan was my second father. In my own mind, I sometimes wonder about the order of those numbers.

* * *

The morning of graduation, there was not a cloud in the sky. I looked around at the other students on that bright, sunny day, and I felt at peace with the world. This was where I was meant to be.

I'd earned a degree in geology and enough education credits to obtain my teaching certificate. Family and friends had come to see me graduate from college, something they probably never imagined I'd do. My old junior high in Baytown had hired me to teach science the following fall, an amazing turn of events. Our house was sold, the car was packed, and we were ready to start a new life.

A Kiowa Indian spoke to our graduating class. His nation had adopted our university because we were the Midwestern Indians, and he was there to give each of us the title of honorary Kiowa Indian.

He said, "You have been studying in the world of books and you have completed your studies. Congratulations.

"Now you are about to enter other worlds. One is the world of nature. If you find the world of nature and the world of books disagreeing, believe in nature."

I have held that truth in my heart for more than fifty years.

The Harrington boys, 1943
(L to R) Happy, Raleigh and Glenn

High School Senior Pictures, 1951
Glenn Harrington and Melva Maley

Glenn, Football, 1951

Melva, Drum Majorette, 1951

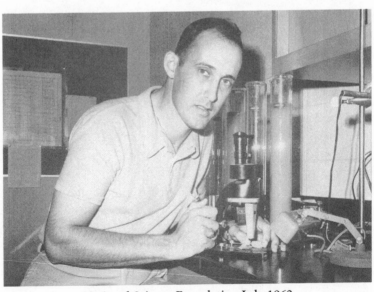

National Science Foundation Lab, 1962

Honeymoon in Mexico, 1951

Wichita Falls, Texas, 1952

1968, The Harrington Family at the end of hiking
330 miles in 33 days on the "The John Muir Trail."
(L to R) Beth, Melva, Glenn, Tina and Marsha.

Cutting our wedding cake, December 22, 1951

Wichita Falls, Texas, 1952

Park Ranger Naturalist, Rocky Mountain National Park, 1991

At the wedding of our daughter Tina Gale, 1988

Memorial Day celebration, Grand Lake, CO, 2007

Family Picture, 1971
(L to R) Beth, Melva, Glenn, Tina and Marsha

CHAPTER 7

Teacher

We pulled out of Wichita Falls the next day, heading east. The sun was in our faces, rising on our new life. From now on, things were going to be different from anything we'd experienced in the past.

After we'd ridden in silence for a while, our two precious daughters watching the scenery go by out the windows of our 1952 Ford Custom four-door, a six-by-eight-foot trailer humming along behind us packed to the gills with our things, I turned to Melva. "How much money do we have left?" I asked, feeling a sense of pride that all our bills were settled and all our loans were paid. She dug around a little, counted the notes and change in her purse, then looked over with a little smile and said, "We have almost $100."

It might not have been much, but all things considered, we felt rich.

* * *

Soon we were settled in Baytown and my new teaching job was about to begin. In some ways, it was surreal. Here I was, back in my hometown, preparing to teach in a school where I'd struggled to find my place in the world. I thought long and hard about those years, what they'd given me and what I'd been denied. I set a goal for myself that I would do my best not to let my students feel the shame I'd felt in school when I was their age. I'd teach my students to think for themselves, to do the best they could according to their individual abilities so that when they walked out of my classroom for the last time they would have faith knowing they would be okay in their life after school.

In a lot of ways, it was the little things that made that possible.

Because of my reading problem, it was difficult for me to pronounce names, but saying each student's name correctly was something that was important to me in order to establish a respectful relationship with the boys and girls in my classes. I had to get it right the first time. So as soon as the list of my new students was available, I took it home and went over it with Melva. Soon I had the reputation of being good at pronouncing names, even though that was far from the truth.

Every class period I would stand at the classroom door as the students filed in, greeting each one by name. It wasn't long before they returned my greetings and we'd established a rapport that made a difference in my role as an instructor and their attitude in my class. I always said, "Yes, sir" and "Yes, ma'am" to my students too, because I felt that if I respected them first, they would return that respect to me.

Because of my problem with spelling, I couldn't write on the blackboard in front of the students. Instead, just like in the Air Force, I would arrive early to class and draw diagrams of the scientific concepts we were covering that day; if I were giving a quiz I would carefully copy it onto the board, then pull down the map above it to cover it up. I taught a wide variety of science courses in those years—life science, biology, earth science, historical geology, chemistry, physics, and physical geology. I used very few tests that required long written answers because I could not read them. Instead, my exams were made up of multiple choice and true-or-false questions, as well as diagrams the students would label or complete. I could grade these tests easily, and the students mastered the concepts just as well, and perhaps even better, with this format.

Just like at Sheppard Air Force Base, I passed along my way of learning—visually, with in-depth discussion and hands-on exercises—to my students. I incorporated lots of labs, which made science real for the kids and also made it fun. Science fairs and projects were always part of my curriculum; so were games and puzzles and exercises to teach them how to think, not just regurgitate the concepts we covered. Once I brought in a clock to class that had all the numbers arranged counterclockwise, with hands that moved counterclockwise too. I wanted the kids' minds to grasp new possibilities and ways of thinking they might not have considered before. I'd also challenge them with brainteasers, games of strategy like checkers and chess, and "What if?" games that had no right or wrong answers. There was something for every level of thinking, and everyone was involved.

I found that the students were interested in talking and knowing more about how to think. Some of the kids with the lowest grades were the most involved in discussions and games, which underscored what I'd come to learn myself: reading is a great asset, but it is not a requirement for learning. Being engaged and using your mind in a variety of ways is.

I also did something for my students that I'd always wished had been done for me when I was young: I made myself available to them. In the upper corner of the blackboard in my classroom I'd write my home phone number in very large handwriting, about two feet long and six inches high. I told the girls and boys that it was okay to call me if they had questions about our class or school. That way, they had no excuse for not knowing what we'd covered or what homework they were responsible for. In my eyes, if a student got an F in my class for not learning, then I got an F for not teaching.

* * *

In those years discipline was handled much differently than it is today. Especially in my early days as a teacher, paddling was an acceptable form of punishment, and I was given that responsibility as part of my job.

After a couple of years of paddling kids as the main form of discipline, the school heard of a new way to deal with disruptive students, a method called reality therapy. Instead of corporal punishment, a questioning technique was used to help children consider their actions and learn from them.

The school sent me to the University of Houston to learn more about this technique, and I watched firsthand how much more effective it was to question kids and get them to think as opposed to hitting them with a paddle.

Here's how it worked: Say a boy disturbed his class by throwing his books on the floor. He'd be sent to my office (I was the boys' counselor in those years), and the conversation would go something like this:

"Joey, what did you do that you shouldn't have done?"

If Joey took ownership for his actions, he'd say, "I threw my books on the floor and that was wrong. I shouldn't have done that."

But if Joey wasn't willing to own up to his bad behavior, the next thing that happened was something he didn't expect. I would say in a calm voice, "That's fine, Joey. If you don't want to talk to me about what you did that you shouldn't have done, that's okay. Please sit down and think about your actions, and if you decide you want to talk, just let me know."

There was a small room next to my office that I could see into through my open door. In the middle of the room sat a folding metal chair.

It wouldn't take long, usually four or five minutes, and Joey would start waving at me that he was ready to talk. "Mr. Harrington," he'd say as I entered the room, "I threw my books on the floor, and I shouldn't have done that."

"That's good of you to admit that, Joey," I'd reply, and after a few more questions, Joey would be back in class. In most cases I wouldn't see children like Joey in my office again. This new program worked because we had found a better way.

But there's a little more to the story than appears on the surface. Remember that folding metal chair Joey sat in while he thought about his bad behavior? Well, what he didn't know was that I had used a hacksaw to cut the front legs of the chair about an inch shorter than the back legs. Then I cleaned the seat with furniture polish to make it as slippery as possible. Though the chair looked okay, anyone sitting in it had to fight to keep from ending up on the floor. After three or four minutes, the unsuspecting child's legs would start to cramp, then his back. Within a minute or two more, he was ready to talk and leave that slippery, tortuous chair behind.

* * *

I began teaching in the fall of 1958, and it wasn't long after that dramatic social and historical events began to take place that affected everyone in the country, including the students in small Baytown, Texas, where I lived and taught.

One day will stick with me forever: November 22, 1963. It was a Friday afternoon, lunch was over, and the children in my class were taking a test. I always had a radio on while the students took an exam; the soft background music had a calming effect that helped ease any anxiety they might feel on test-taking days. During college, when I studied late in the evening or early in the morning, I had always turned on the radio to keep myself company. Filling the silence helped me focus and kept me from being distracted, and I saw it had the same effect with my classes after I became a teacher.

The kids were working away when two students began talking. I went over to tell them to be quiet and one said in a firm voice, "Mr. Harrington, you need to hear what's on the radio."

I leaned in to the radio in time to hear, "The president of the United States has been assassinated."

I stood there for a few moments, shocked, developing a plan of action. My course set, the first thing I did was whisper to a young man, "Go to the office and tell the principal to come to Mr. Harrington's room now. You tell him Mr. Harrington said now."

As soon as the student left I stopped the test, collected the papers, and told the class what was happening.

Until the principal arrived in my classroom, he was unaware that President Kennedy had been shot. A few minutes after we spoke, his voice came over the PA system announcing to the student body and faculty what had happened in Dallas.

My 1:00 class stayed in my classroom for the rest of the day. We listened to the radio and discussed President Kennedy's assassination. It was important, letting my students talk. They were calm as I allowed them to participate in this historic event, a day we would hold in our memories for the rest of our lives.

Another major event that happened in those years was integration.

It was 1968, and I had been assigned to Horace Mann Junior High. The school had just begun to integrate, and the violence we had seen throughout the South as states began desegregating schools made our district cautious about what might happen in southeast Texas.

I was chosen to be on the Community Committee to Oversee Integration along with five other men. Our purpose was to brief and give recommendations to the school board about problems or complaints in regard to integrating the area schools.

We were lucky. Integration came to our school district without problems. The children who joined our student body and the faculty who taught them benefited from our blended classrooms, and after three meetings, the committee disbanded.

* * *

When I had been at Horace Mann for five years, I accepted a part-time position at Lee Junior College teaching night courses in geology. The job included teaching on weekends at the Department of Corrections in Huntsville, Texas—an interesting development in my career.

Teaching inmates was one of the more interesting jobs I ever had. The inmates weren't in prison because they weren't smart; they were there because they'd made a mistake. I found them to be good students.

They also had a sense of humor. One night, while teaching about geological time and time in general, I said that my life was limited by how much time I had and that if I had more time, I could do more things.

An inmate raised his hand and said, "Mr. Harrington, I have fifteen years I'll be happy to give you."

Humor was a part of my interaction with my younger students too. One day during the time I was teaching junior high, a group of kids came into my room from another teacher's class and were complaining about her. As soon as class started, we discussed the situation as a group. I told them that when something happens that you think isn't fair, you shouldn't get angry, you should be nice to the person you're upset with. With that option presented to them, they all decided that the next day each student, all twenty-eight of them, would bring an apple to the teacher in question.

It worked. The next day when she came into her class and saw twenty-eight apples on her desk, everything was made right. The whole class had a good laugh over it and that was the end of that. Or so I thought.

Just a day later, when I arrived in my classroom after lunch, I could see that my students were excited. I couldn't figure out why until I looked up and saw my desk. There, piled on top, were twenty-eight onions. The kids and some faculty members who had just happened to stop by thought it was hilarious. I did too.

Our apples and onions ended up being a good lesson about kindness as well as about healthy interactions between students and teachers. That weekend I planted those onions in the flower bed in front of the school, and a few months later teachers, students, custodians, and even parents were cutting onion tops and having a ball.

* * *

The small communities I worked in made it easy for me to develop a positive attitude toward teaching, and to do it well. Sure, it took me longer to get ready for class than it took the other teachers, but that was okay with me. I was always prepared, and I could see that my enthusiasm for science rubbed off on my students, no matter what their age.

Being deeply involved with the entire student body at every school in which I worked allowed me to relate to the students, faculty, and parents. In addition to teaching, I also held roles as student council advisor, school bus driver, football and track coach, and science fair coordinator. I became a part of my kids' lives beyond the classroom, which helped them see how much their success meant to me. The respect I gave to them they gave right back. My students named me teacher of the year, and their parents included my name in the *Who's Who Among America's Teachers*.

With pride I realized I had become the teacher I'd always wanted to have myself.

CHAPTER 8

The Spirit of the Mountains

When I first saw the Rocky Mountains at the age of twenty-seven, I fell deeply in love. I stepped into a world of glacier-gouged canyons, of seemingly endless forests, meadows, lakes, and streams. The cool, thin air filled me with energy, especially when dramatic summer storms raced across the tundra, leaving fog, rainbows, and even a skiff of snow in their wake.

It was 1960, I had just finished my second year of teaching, and I was spending my summer working as a ranger-naturalist in Rocky Mountain National Park.

In the years since my childhood days building forts and tree houses in the woods near my family home or exploring the bayou in Mermentau, I had never lost my love for the outdoors. Surrounding myself with natural beauty always gave me a sense of peace and belonging to something larger than myself, whether it was the mystery of a swamp shaded by moss-covered cypress and filled with the sounds of wetland creatures or the vastness of an open prairie, bright with sunlight and the gentle movement of swaying grass. Until my first summer in Colorado I had never seen a sky so impossibly blue or mountain peaks that reached altitudes too high for trees to grow. The valleys and steep slopes were carpeted with wildflowers, and herds of elk, deer, and bighorn sheep grazed there undisturbed. Each day I would see something new and amazing that would ignite my scientific curiosity about the plants and animals of this extreme ecosystem.

I wondered what I had done to deserve a job that felt more like a summer away at camp than something I was being paid for.

Rocky Mountain National Park was not my first assignment with the National Park Service. During my first year of teaching, I had pondered what I might do during the months when school was out. I landed on the idea of becoming an NPS interpreter. It would be a great way to combine my love of teaching and the outdoors, in addition to creating memorable summers with my growing young family. I applied to several parks, and we got a job at Sequoia, in the Sierra Nevada in central California. Our little tent house— two rooms with a canvas roof, cold running water, two bare light bulbs for light and a woodstove for cooking and heat—sat on the west side of the park, near a grove of giant sequoias called Grant Grove.

Beth and Marsha fell in love with the giant sequoias, majestic and special because they are among the oldest and largest living things on earth. The park was the greatest backyard any child could ask for. At ages seven and five, the girls were eager to try hiking, and soon we were on the trail every week, with long trips around the Rays Lake Loop, each girl with her own backpack.

Now I was experiencing my next adventure, this time alone and in a much different mountain terrain. Instead of millennium-old sequoias, in the Rockies ponderosa pine, Douglas fir, and aspen dotted the landscape near my little trailer, with wind-twisted spruce and fir at tree line. I gazed in awe at the landscape, wishing my family were there to enjoy it with me. Melva was home with Beth and Marsha, plus a brand-new addition to the family: little Tina Gale, born June 12, 1960, right before I left for Colorado. Melva and I had agreed that I should go to the Rocky Mountains without her and the girls since her parents and mine were right there in Baytown to help out with our new baby daughter.

So there I was, breathing in the clear, cool Colorado mountain air, just happy to be alive. Every morning that summer I would shine my shoes, press my uniform shirt, adjust my tie and ranger hat just so, and with a mechanical counter in my pocket make it my goal to talk to at least two hundred people a day. I meandered through the restaurants, shops, and along the shoreline of Grand Lake, on the park's western edge, mingling with visitors, answering their questions, and giving them hiking and camping tips.

During the day I also led nature walks, hiking up to four miles with small groups of visitors while discussing the natural history of the area. At night I put on campfire programs complete with songs and storytelling. I had to study the geology, ecology, and history of the area, but I never had to read in front of others, and if I had to write a report for my supervisor, a secretary helped me turn my handwritten version into a typewritten paper, kindly and quietly correcting my misspellings and grammar mistakes as she transcribed.

* * *

Evening campfire programs were a highlight of my time at Rocky Mountain National Park.

I'd been assigned to Timber Creek, a small campground at the upper end of a glacier-carved valley at an elevation of about nine thousand feet. There were only a hundred campsites there, so the setting for my programs was pretty primitive, with no amphitheater, electricity, or speaker stand, just a fire pit down by the creek.

I would always arrive about two hours before the program was scheduled to begin. I drove a green park service Ford F-Series pickup with a load of wood and a can of kerosene in the back. I'd stack the wood real tight in the fire pit so the fire would last at least an hour, then, when no one was watching, soak it down with kerosene.

After building my fire but before lighting it, I'd head down to the lower end of the campground and visit every occupied campsite to introduce myself and invite campers to that evening's program. On different nights I covered different topics, sometimes talking about the geology of the Rockies, other times discussing the human history of the area, and sometimes covering the plants and animals visitors were likely to see. I'd tell campers to bring their folding chairs, flashlights, and a blanket to keep warm, since at that elevation it was bound to be chilly in the evening, even in July or August.

As large and small families and young and old couples arrived at the fire pit, the sound of the bubbling creek accompanied their laughter and comfortable chatter while they settled in for an hour of entertainment. That was my cue to light the fire, so with the strike of a single match I set the wood aflame. Often I would hear whispers from the crowd: "Did you see that? He lit all that wood with just one match!" But I always kept my secret weapon—the kerosene—to myself.

As the cool night air descended and my presentation began, I felt a closeness of spirit among my small audience. They listened to my talk, laughed at my jokes, and joined in with questions about the park and stories of things they had seen during their visit. No matter how many times I heard the same anecdotes, I always interjected, "Is that right?" or "Wow, I never heard anything like that before!"

It didn't cost me anything to listen to their stories, and I enjoyed seeing the expressions on their faces as they relived these memorable events in their lives.

Soon the flames of my fire would be reduced to warm, glowing coals and people would huddle close together under their blankets. Before they headed off for bed, I'd pull out my five-string banjo for some campfire songs to end the night.

The most requested song was the old Gene Autry tune "When It's Springtime in the Rockies." It's a slow song that a lot of people knew back then, and they enjoyed it because it reminded them of where they were. I always saved it for last. After a verse or two, I'd start slowing down the tempo and lowering the volume to focus on the emotion of the song more than its words. Under a dark sky crowded with stars, the soft music washed over us, calling forth the spirit of the mountains and bringing us a sense of peace.

* * *

In later summers, Melva and the girls joined me again, and we returned to Sequoia. Not far from our little cabin, off the beaten track, was the stump of a giant sequoia tree that had been cut down before the area was a national park. It was called the Centennial Stump, not because it was a hundred years old—it was much, much older than that—but because a sixteen-foot section of the tree had been taken to the Centennial International Exhibition of 1876, the first world's fair held in the United States, in Philadelphia. The fair was named for the one hundredth anniversary of the Declaration of Independence.

No one knew the age of the tree when it was cut down, so I was given the special assignment of counting the rings of the stump, which was twenty-nine feet in diameter.

With a tree that big you can't just start counting rings—it's too easy to lose your place. There's a special method for figuring out the tree's age, and it requires two simple tools: a pocketknife with a sharp point and a box of wooden kitchen matches.

First you take about thirty of those matches and, using your knife, cut off each match head and sharpen the end into a wedge. Next, you begin counting the rings from the outside of the stump using the sharp point of your knife to keep your place. When you've counted a hundred rings, you make a hole with the knife tip and insert the wedge end of a match. This makes it easy to survey your work and know just how many rings you've counted: ten matches equals a thousand rings. When I was about three feet from the center of the stump, I set my twentieth match. That's when I stopped.

Looking at that match, I realized something profound: it represented a time two thousand years ago. I was looking at the tree ring that was growing the year Christ was born.

I paused for a while to think about the significance of that marker. Before my very eyes I could see the point in history that shifted from being before Christ to after His birth. For the tree, that year made little difference: the rings before and after looked pretty much the same. It struck me that the natural world had made little note of an event that had completely changed our social, religious, and spiritual world forever. I couldn't help but think back to the wise words of my college commencement speaker and feel the power of nature in this one example before me.

And amazingly, I still had three more feet and hundreds of rings to go. This very tree was six feet in diameter the day Christ was born.

When I finished my task, I wrote up a report for the National Park Service files giving the official age of the Centennial tree: at the time it was cut down, it was 2,522 years old.

* * *

When you consider a living thing that's older than Christianity, philosophical questions start to crowd your brain. Sometimes during my campfire programs, I'd find myself put on the spot by just such questions, so I learned to think fast in order to answer them.

One night, it was a little girl who stumped me. Now sometimes when someone asks you a question you just don't know the answer to—maybe nobody does—you can glaze over it by pretending you didn't hear. But this child had a loud, clear voice, and everyone sitting around her heard her question. I had no choice but to answer.

She asked this: "Where did the first sequoia tree come from?"

Well.

I started slowly, buying time. "Young lady, that's a very good question," I said. "Thank you for asking that."

And suddenly, inspiration struck.

"When God created this world, he created everything with a purpose and for a reason. It is possible, just possible, that giant sequoia trees, the ones you have asked about, were the very last things He created on this earth.

"Now the reason I can say that is that giant sequoias are different from any other tree and any other living thing. First of all, every plant and animal on this earth has a life span, which means that they only live for so long and then they die from old age. That is the law of nature, and there is no exception to that law—except with the giant sequoia.

"We have never known a giant sequoia to die of old age, and some live for 3,500 or even 4,000 years. They don't die during a forest fire because their bark is very thick and does not burn. They don't die from insect infestation because they produce sap that contains tannic acid, and the insects stay away from it. They may be blown over during a windstorm, but that's because they have a shallow root system. They just don't die from being old.

"So when you ask where the first sequoia tree came from, I'd have to say it came from God. Tomorrow, when you are walking among the giant sequoias, stop for a moment and think about that. Look around you, and realize that when you are standing in a grove of sequoias, you are standing in a great cathedral."

The next morning my supervisor, who happened to be at the campfire program the night before to evaluate me, asked me why I didn't bring up the evolution of the tree in answer to the little girl's question. I didn't really try to answer him, though. All I could hear as he was speaking was the sound of the other campers' soft applause after I told my story.

* * *

When you're a park ranger living in the Sierra Nevada, you do a lot of hiking and climbing. But no matter how much you do, it seems there is always a longer trail or a higher mountain to climb. That's what got Melva and me interested in hiking Mount Whitney.

Mount Whitney is the highest mountain in the lower 48 states, at an elevation of 14,496.811 feet above sea level. It's located on the eastern side of the Sierra Nevada and on the western side of Death Valley. We liked the idea of being able to say, "There is no mountain higher than the one I have climbed." It reinforced that we could go beyond our limits, physically and in other areas of our lives.

And so we packed the car, left the girls with another park ranger's family, and drove the five hours to Death Valley to climb to the highest point in the continental United States.

There are two ways you can think about climbing a mountain. One is to ask permission of the mountain, and the other is to defy it from stopping you. We chose to ask permission, and approached the climb with humility and respect.

The first day, we hiked nine miles with an elevation gain of five thousand feet. When we were two miles from the summit, bad weather set in, forcing us to take cover. The tricky part was that we were above tree line, so the only shelter available was under a very large boulder. Fortunately, there was just enough room beneath it for our two sleeping bags, so that's where we spent the night.

As we lay huddled together in the darkness, we listened to the rain and watched the lightning strike overhead. Between booms of thunder, we could hear rockslides coming down the mountainside, some very close by. The crashing echoed against the walls of our tiny rock shelter. Other creatures must have heard it too, because soon we discovered we had visitors: a family of mice. But it turned out they didn't care about the storm, they just wanted the food inside our backpacks. To keep it from their hungry little mouths, we stuffed candy bars and sandwiches deep in our sleeping bags and waited out the storm from our high mountain perch.

Finally the sky cleared, the rain stopped, and we crawled out from beneath our boulder and into the first light of day. Death Valley was still dark below us, but the sky above was clear and bright. At 14,000 feet, when you look straight up the sky appears more black than blue. It was an incredible sight.

We packed up, and soon were climbing over and around the rocks we had heard falling during the night. At about 9:00 that morning, we reached the top of Mount Whitney.

From the benchmark at the summit, we could look down nearly three miles to a valley that is more than two hundred feet below sea level. As we stood there, each of us silently thanked the mountain for allowing us passage.

I knew we didn't have long before we needed to start our descent, so I stood still, taking in the vista laid out before me. But all of a sudden, I could see out of the corner of my eye that Melva was up to something. I turned and was surprised to see my wife stacking rocks into a pile about two feet high. Satisfied by her work, she climbed on top. Melva was now standing two feet taller than the highest mountain in the lower 48. This lady never stops amazing me.

By then it was 10:00, and we had eleven miles to hike if we were going to make it out that day. We'd have to let those few minutes on top of Mount Whitney last us a lifetime. We started down the trail.

By keeping a steady pace we were able to reach the car by 5:00 that afternoon. The challenge of the 5,700-foot ascent and the joy of the descent filled us with the pride of our accomplishment. It was then we understood that a mountain doesn't let you get by with excuses. When you determine you will climb it, you have to do it on your true merits, not on who you wish you could be.

Climbing Mount Whitney was the crowning achievement of our summer. Soon after, we returned to Baytown. But I brought home with me the excitement of the Sierras, and a story or two of our adventures.

In my heart, I felt I was finally reaching the top of a mountain I had always wanted to climb.

CHAPTER 9
The Launch of *Sputnik*

B BEEP – BEEP – BEEP.

As I drove across Chisnos Basin in Big Bend National Park on a fall day in October of 1957, the sounds of *Sputnik*, hurtling through space high above me, came to Earth, transmitted through my car radio.

The Russians had just put the first satellite into space. Each time it rounded the globe its sound was recorded and sent out over the airwaves. That faint BEEP-BEEP-BEEP put all Americans who heard it on notice: the space race had begun, and the United States had found itself in the unusual predicament of playing catch-up.

I was on a geologic field trip in southwest Texas when I first heard the broadcast. Little did I know the influence that event would have on my life. News of *Sputnik* would launch our country into the new frontier of space exploration. I would be carried forward on that journey too, into territory I'd never known I could explore.

* * *

Once the Russians had put a satellite into orbit, the U.S. government realized that it needed to act fast to accelerate its own space program. The first step was to improve the science curriculum in classrooms from junior high on up to create the scientists who could rise to this great challenge. In the late 1950s, with that goal in mind the National Science Foundation began offering grants to send science teachers back to college to improve their teaching. When word came to my Baytown classroom that the government was offering money so teachers like me could return to college, it got me to thinking. Maybe I could qualify. Maybe I could earn a master's degree too.

But as in the past, doubts overshadowed me. My first thought was naturally my reading. During my four years in the military, my years at Midwestern, and while I was teaching, it hadn't improved. I still read at about the fourth-grade level. And yet I'd succeeded at all the things I'd tried. It had taken commitment and sacrifice, but the reward had proven to be greater than the struggle.

Melva and I spent many hours discussing what going to graduate school would mean for us. Taking on this challenge meant we'd have to leave our families and set up house in a new town, now with two young children and another one on the way. She would be primarily responsible for taking care of the girls and our home while I went to class and studied, and be there to help me, a functioning dyslexic doing graduate-level work. Money might be tight, like it had been in Wichita Falls. But Melva knew how important my quest for knowledge was—unlike anyone else in my life—and she supported me. She said yes.

And so in 1959, after we returned from our first summer in Sequoia, I decided to see if I could get into graduate school. I got a list of all the universities that were offering a master's program in geology, and that winter, I applied to all of them.

Weeks passed. I didn't hear a thing. It was getting near the end of the school year, and I was beginning to think that maybe this idea of getting a master's degree was a pipe dream after all. At Cedar Bay Junior High, where I was teaching that year, my classroom was across the hall from the school counselor's office. One Friday afternoon at the end of May, Mrs. Martin crossed the hall and knocked on my door. I had a phone call. Did I want to take it while she watched my class?

I strolled into her office and picked up the phone. It was a Dr. Vaughn from the University of South Dakota, and he was calling to let me know I'd been accepted to their graduate program in geology. I sat there for a moment, thinking about what this meant. I had been offered a chance, and that was all I needed.

As I walked back to my classroom, there was a faint sound ringing in my ears. It was the BEEP-BEEP-BEEP of *Sputnik* passing over me, high above the Earth.

* * *

That summer we welcomed a new addition, Tina Gale, to our family; I spent a glorious season at Rocky Mountain National Park, and then I came home to help Melva pack up for our move to South Dakota. Just a few days before the fall semester was about to start, we arrived in Vermillion in our 1958 blue four-door Chevy Delray with three beautiful little girls in the backseat. When I asked Melva how much money she had in her purse to help us start our new lives, she counted it up and told me. It was just under $100.

The University of South Dakota is located in far southeastern South Dakota on a bluff above the Missouri River. Lewis and Clark stopped here on their expedition west and shot their first buffalo on the plains nearby. It's a rural community, but Vermillion also boasts one of the state's major universities, with the only law school and medical school in South Dakota. That combination of rural and academic was the perfect mix for our family, and the perfect place for me to complete my studies as a graduate student.

We rented a farmhouse in a small Swedish community about ten miles north of town. Our oldest daughter, Beth, attended a one-room schoolhouse a hundred yards from our front door. The girls loved living on a farm, spending time with our neighbors Ray and Roselle Nelson and their three young children, and living out this new adventure in a new part of the country. Melva loved it too, and our house was filled with the sounds of female chatter and laughter.

Classes started, and I returned to my old learning program of listening, taking careful notes, and asking lots of questions. I wasn't sure how I was going to cover up my poor reading in class but, strangely enough, in graduate school that didn't seem to be a big problem. I had to work harder and longer than the other students to prepare, but in our labs and during class time I was competing head to head with the other students. Part of the reason was the setting: we would sit around a table or a lab bench and talk about what we were studying, and then go off to do our individual experiments.

In two or three hours we'd meet back to discuss the results. It was a constant flow of learning, working, and discovering new things. Although the professors sometimes gave us a short test that we used collectively to evaluate our work, there were very few exams to take or papers to write.

Something was happening that I didn't understand at first. The material was much more advanced than in my undergraduate courses, and yet it was easier. I didn't feel the constant struggle that I'd felt during my years at Midwestern. I was earning a 3.98 GPA.

Pretty soon I realized what the difference was. It was the National Science Foundation grant. The energy I had spent trying to work and go to school at the same time had drained me as an undergraduate. At USD, my grant not only covered my tuition, books, and supplies, it also paid me a salary higher than what I'd earned as a teacher. In fact, one of the conditions of the grant was that I couldn't be employed while I was a student. For the first time in my college career, I could devote myself fully to my studies.

My new challenge was finding a quiet place to do my work in a bustling household filled with the sounds of three small girls. I discovered the best time to study was early in the morning, so I started getting up earlier and earlier—first 5:00, then 4:00, then 3:00—to do my work. I had a small desk in the corner of our dining room that I called my "altar to higher education." It had everything I needed, arranged just so: books, papers, and a yellow pad in the middle, a coffeepot to the right, a gooseneck lamp to the left, and a small Philco radio in between.

In those silent pre-dawn hours the first thing I would do was make coffee. Then I'd set my coffeepot on its wire stand with a small candle burning underneath it and dole out portions into a little white Cajun cup so the coffee was always warm. The green plastic Philco radio was tuned to an AM station that faded in and out. It kept me company when everyone else in the house was fast asleep.

In addition to working in the early morning hours, I'd find ways to sneak in study time whenever I had a spare moment. One trick I had was to review my notes while driving. I was still using note cards with condensed notes on them, and I'd prop the cards on the dashboard while I drove. In retrospect this might not have been the safest method, but my route to and from the university was on a country road with very little traffic; those twenty extra minutes of study time helped me ready myself for the day.

* * *

Students in the Geology Department took a lot of field trips as part of our graduate program. We would go to the Badlands to collect fossils and study paleontology and to the Black Hills to study hard rock geology. For someone like me who loved hands-on learning, being out in the field and seeing the past laid out before me, like a giant puzzle I needed to solve, quenched my thirst for knowledge like no textbook ever could.

Sometimes I would take our family along to dig up the past, and other times I'd go by myself in our Volkswagen van camper. It was on one of those lone trips, in the summer of 1961, that I had an experience I'll never forget.

I was headed to the western side of the state to look for fossils in the Badlands. My first stop was Rapid City, where they had a city museum with geology specimens and Sioux Indian artifacts in its collections. I thought this would be a good place to start—seeing where people had found fossils in the past and talking to the geologists on staff could lead me to some good digging spots. While I was inside, I overheard an old Indian lady trying to sell the museum a buffalo robe. They weren't interested in the robe, but I was interested in what she might know about the area, so when she left I followed her outside. My instinct was right: she told me there were lots of fossils near where she lived, on the Oglala Sioux Reservation near the White River, and she gave me her name and directions to her house. I wrote it all down, thanked her, and following her instructions, headed southeast on State Highway 18.

When you're hunting for fossils a bad road is usually a good sign. When I turned off the main highway onto a dirt road, crossed a cattle guard, and started following an un-graded wagon trail, I figured I was in for some real treasures. Every now and then, there'd be a split in the road and I would do what I've done many times in my life: take the road less traveled. After about twelve miles, just as her directions said, I came to a small white house on the prairie next to the White River. It had a windmill, a small corral, and about ten skinny cows. It belonged to the old Indian woman, Mrs. Bessanette.

Mr. Bessanette came out into the yard and we talked for a long time standing by my Volkswagen. When the subject turned to fossils, his eyes lit up. Several years before he had walked up on a fossil that was nine steps long and four steps wide, he told me, but he had never been able to find it again. He also described a section of the Badlands about a mile south of his place where there was a big hole in the ground full of fossils, and that lit my eyes up too. When I asked if he would give me directions, he told me yes, but that I needed to go to the Tribal Council office in Pine Ridge first to get permission to remove fossils from reservation land. In the blink of an eye I decided I would, and thanked Mr. Bessanette for his good advice.

It was getting late, too late to drive to Pine Ridge, so Mr. Bessanette offered to let me camp by his house for the night. I was grateful, but also didn't want to overstay my welcome, so instead I told him I would drive my van camper about a hundred yards downstream of where they lived and camp there.

It was then, as I was getting back into the Volkswagen, that I noticed Mr. Bessanette's daughter, who looked to be about twelve, watching us from the house. I'd bought two Texas watermelons from a truck at the side of the road on my way out of Rapid City, and seeing her small face in the window gave me an idea: as thanks for their generosity, I would offer one to her. I asked Mr. Bessanette if he would call her outside so I could give her a gift. Shyly, she stepped out of their small home and waited by her father while I opened the van to retrieve my offering.

I handed over the round melon expecting her face to light up with delight, but instead she just stood there, wordlessly. Her questioning eyes darted from me to her father and back again. Finally, Mr. Bessanette said softly, "She doesn't know what that is. She's never seen a watermelon before."

My gesture had backfired. I was sure I had embarrassed the poor girl. Mr. Bessanette said something to his daughter in Sioux and she took the melon and went into the house. Later that evening, when she'd had her first bite of that cool, sweet melon, perhaps she would forgive me.

The sun was hanging low in the sky and it was time for me to set up camp for the night. I wished Mr. Bessanette good night, and then headed down to the river. Just as I was washing the last of my supper dishes, however, the Indian walked up with a determined step. He didn't stay long, but what he said was interesting because it was the only reason he had come down, and that was to tell me what he knew about fossils.

"I know you are from the university and you know fossils," he said, "but I know fossils too, I know where all these fossils came from." Naturally, I was interested to hear the rest. "I know how to read, I read my Bible, and I know about the great flood," Mr. Bessanette told me next. "I know all the animals on the earth could not get on the ark, and those that couldn't get on drowned, and that is where all these fossils came from."

There was a pause. I looked down at the ground for a second, then squarely into the eyes of this man with dark, heavily lined skin, straight jet-black hair, high cheekbones, and no hat. Then I spoke with respect. "You're right, Mr. Bessanette, that's where all these fossils came from." He seemed pleased, and nodded. "I knew it," he said simply. Standing there on the banks of the White River in the late afternoon, we shared the moment, a Sioux Indian of many years and a young scientist, respecting each other's ideas.

The next day I was up early and on my way to Pine Ridge to get the collecting permit. But first I went by Mr. Bessanette's place to see if there was anything I could get him in town since I could see they didn't have a car. He was in the corral with the cows. I'd noticed how skinny his cattle were when I drove up the day before, but seeing them now up close told me they were in serious trouble. Two had what is called drop tail—they were not getting enough minerals from their diet, so they had begun to absorb the calcium in their tails, and the tails had come unjointed. When I mentioned this and asked the old Sioux if I could help, he said there was an Indian agency in Pine Ridge, and if I would go by and tell them who I was they would give me sacks of minerals for his cows.

So that was the first thing I did when I got to Pine Ridge. The man at the agency office agreed to give me the minerals, but, according to government rules, he could only give me three sacks at a time. We both knew I needed more, so we came up with a solution: I'd drive around for an hour, come back, and he'd give me an additional three. It took just about an hour for me to go get my collecting permit, head back to the agency office, and pick up the remaining sacks of minerals.

I spent the rest of the morning and afternoon tracking down that hole in the ground Mr. Bessanette had told me about. There was no road, no trail to the spot, just buffalo grass about twelve or eighteen inches high and not very thick. But his directions were good, and I found the big hole without much trouble. He wasn't kidding when he said it was big: it was about a half mile across, a mile and a half long, and at least 125 feet deep.

I took my pack, a small shovel, and a rock hammer and climbed on in. The floor of the hole was surprisingly flat and easy to walk on. And just like Mr. Bessanette said, it was full of fossils. I found mammal heads and backbones from creatures that had lived millions of years ago. I also found fossils of turtle shells, some sitting on top of rock pedestals formed when the soft stone had weathered away around them. Because there was so much to choose from, I picked only the best specimens and started carrying them up to the Volkswagen, working at this until dark. In what seemed like no time, the sky above me was filled with stars and I headed up to my van with my last haul, fixed a simple supper, then spent the night along the lip of this ancient treasure trove.

The next morning I woke early. I wanted to share my finds with someone I knew would appreciate them as much as I did. As the sun broke over the horizon Mr. Bessanette's house came into view through the VW's windshield, and before I had turned off the engine, he was standing next to the van. I pushed open the doors and displayed those ancient fossils. Silently we stood there, admiring, then wished each other well and said goodbye.

* * *

My graduate school program lasted a year, so it seemed like almost no time before I was studying for final exams.

There are two tests you have to pass in order to receive a master's degree: a written and an oral. The written test came first, and I left it feeling confident. Next up were orals. This was the part I looked forward to most: sitting in a room with three of my professors, discussing geology and being quizzed out loud. No reading, no writing, just an hour of discussion. It suited me just fine.

Part of my exam was being able to identify minerals using only their reflection and refraction of light. After I identified several without a hitch, one of the professors asked, "What mineral has an index of refraction of 1.458 and an index of reflection of 1.45?"

I surprised him when I replied, "None."

The professor had inverted the last two numbers for the refraction. It should have been 1.54, which would have been the common mineral quartz. At that point one of the other professors said, "Who is quizzing who here?" and we all laughed.

I passed my orals on the first try and went on to receive my master's degree.

* * *

The morning of graduation, Melva dressed the girls up and put on her Sunday best. I slipped my gown over my best suit, carefully arranged my cap on my head, and turned to look at my family proudly. It had been twelve months of hard work, but we had done it. Our lives had been changed in ways we had not imagined—all because of that BEEP-BEEP-BEEP.

Because we were a thousand miles away from home, our friends and family couldn't come to the ceremony, so we had this moment to ourselves. Melva and the girls sat up in the audience, and I got in line with the other five geology graduate students, ready to go on stage and accept my diploma.

Just as commencement was about to start, I heard something that didn't sound right. It was an attractive young woman in a pretty blue dress coming down the line calling, "Mr. Harrington? Mr. Glenn Harrington?"

I looked up, raising my hand, and she came over and said in a voice loud enough for everyone to hear, "Mr. Harrington, the dean wants to see you."

Suddenly, everything went into slow motion. I felt my knees buckle and my heart start to pound. If the dean had called me out of line that could only mean one thing. But how? Why?

I followed the young woman out of the auditorium and down the hallway to the dean's office. The blue dress that had looked so pretty just a moment ago had lost its luster. The young woman who at first glance appeared so attractive now looked menacing in my eyes.

When I entered his office, the dean was standing there with two other men, all in caps and gowns, and they were talking. I stood there quietly, politely, waiting. Finally the dean turned to me and said, "Mr. Harrington." Then he reached across his desk for a small brown envelope. My heart dropped into my stomach.

It took me a moment to absorb the words that came next, I was so sure I knew what they would be. Instead, the dean said casually, "Here is a telegram somebody sent you. They couldn't find you, so they brought it here instead."

A telegram. For me. I stared at the paper for a moment, took it with a quivering hand, and looked up.

"Sir," I said in a weak voice. "Sir, please don't do that again. Please don't call somebody out of line when they are just about to walk up on stage to receive their diploma. You have no idea what was going through my mind coming up here."

And with that final test passed, I walked down the hall to graduate.

CHAPTER 10
The John Muir Trail

I have always had a hunger to discover some of the truths that hide from us, we who live in modern civilization. Night after night, we lie sheltered inside our homes, forgetting that outside another bed is laid and waiting, in the fields and mountains where God always keeps an open house. John Muir wrote: "Climb the mountains and get their good tidings. Nature's peace will flow into you as sunshine flows into trees. The winds will blow their own freshness into you, and the storms their energy, while cares will drop off like autumn leaves." I have found that to be true—in my hours as a child exploring the shores of Galveston Bay, my summers climbing the high peaks of the American West, and my days roaming the plains in search of evidence of Earth's ancient past.

It was in the spirit of Muir's quote that Melva and I began planning to hike the entire length of the John Muir Trail with our three girls in the summer of 1968. From the Yosemite Valley south to Mount Whitney, the trail follows the Sierra Nevada for 280 miles. We planned to hike it all, plus 50 additional miles back to Sequoia National Park, where we would end our monthlong journey before heading back home to Texas and another school year.

Attempting such a trip isn't something you do lightly: it takes planning, thought, and lots of preparation. The idea had first come to me while working high in the Sierra Nevada. Venturing to its crest several times fueled my desire to go farther and deeper into John Muir's wild mountains—and to bring my family along to receive these mountains' good tidings.

After talking about it for several years, Melva and I got serious about the idea in 1967. Our girls would be old enough to handle the trip by the next summer: Tina Gale would be eight, Marsha eleven, and Beth fourteen (but she would turn fifteen on the trail). To practice, we took long hikes in Sequoia National Park to test ourselves, walking twenty, thirty, even forty miles over the course of several days. We used a mule to carry our gear, and found this was a good way to travel, one that would make a monthlong trip across this rugged terrain possible with all the equipment we would have to bring and the steep climbs in store for us as we headed high into the backcountry.

When we got back home from Sequoia that September, we began planning in earnest, and worked for the next nine months putting the trip together. We corresponded with food suppliers, mule packers, and the park service. We began making lists of everything we would need, studying maps to determine where we would camp and pick up food caches along the trail, considering what we would do if we ran into trouble. Melva and I came up with a "What If?" game for the girls and asked them challenging questions over dinner each night: "What if we are walking down the trail and it starts raining?" "What if there are mosquitos?" "What if someone gets sick?" "What if the mule breaks a leg?" There were lots of right answers to these questions, and soon our daughters were coming up with them—pushing themselves beyond the limits of the comfortable world they inhabited and thinking about the challenges and rewards nature might offer.

As it got close to summer, everyone was ready. We packed our brand-new red-and-white 1967 Ford F-100 with tents and sleeping bags, food and cooking equipment, warm clothes, sturdy shoes, and all the other things we would need for our four-week hike. But there was one glitch. About a month before we were to leave, Beth came to me and said she didn't want to go—she didn't want to leave all her junior high school friends for the summer. We talked about it several times, and I listened to her hesitations, but in the end we decided that she would join us because the trip was already planned and it was too late to change things. I promised Beth that we would do our best to make the trip as fun for her as possible.

When we got to California, there was still a lot to do before we were ready to step into the wilderness. We had to visit several mule packers and give them food caches to take into the Sierras and leave in predetermined locations so we could pick them up as we worked our way down the trail. And then we had to pick up our own mule, a jenny named Lucille.

A mule is one of the noblest products of man: intelligent, powerful, and custom made for mountain travel. Our Lucille was no different. I soon came to admire that 900-pound creature as not only smart and strong, but brave and sweet too. But those who have been around mules will tell you this:

mule management is an imperfect science. They do certain things in certain ways, and each animal's individuality must be respected. From our first day on the trail we saw that this mule was earning our respect by working very, very hard for us, and doing a job that we could not do for ourselves. The least we could do was take good care of her by keeping her well packed, well fed, and well rested.

Day one, June 22, arrived. We woke at 6:00 in our Yosemite Valley campsite, loaded up our four-legged friend, and headed down the trail. Before we'd been hiking a half hour, Marsha saw a bear. Fortunately, it didn't seem to bother our Lucille one bit. But when a string of mules passed us later that morning, she started hurrying us along, determined to follow them nose to tail as she'd been bred to do.

We started across Yosemite Valley, the first in a series of three U-shaped glacial valleys we'd traverse as we headed into the high country. Later we'd cross Kern Valley, and finally, as we reached higher elevations, Lyell. Grassy, broad meadows with streams meandering through made up our landscape, with scrub willows along the stream banks and high talus slopes above.

The first morning on the trail, I led Lucille to a nice patch of grass away from the campground while Melva and the girls started breakfast. When I went to retrieve our mule ten minutes later, she was gone. Mild panic gathered in my stomach. I searched all around—nothing. I called to Melva that I was headed out to find her and took off, following her tracks, without even a moment to change out of my camp moccasins and into tennis shoes. About a half mile up the trail I finally found Lucille, standing by a tree and looking down at me with a gleam in her eye. "Who's in charge here?" she seemed to say. Well, I decided I'd ride this mule back into camp to give her an idea. I made a bridle of her rope, climbed on her back, and nudged her forward with my heels. In fits and starts she moved ahead, then, without warning, kicked up her hind legs and threw me tail over teakettle in a high arc. I landed flat on my back in the dirt and lay there for a moment looking up at the cloudless sky. I'd learned my lesson: Lucille had her own ideas about this trip, just as I had mine.

Several times on our trip I came to the conclusion that Lucille was not only more intelligent than I, but braver, stronger, and more coordinated. Instead of waging constant war against her, I decided to solicit her cooperation.

I wrapped her rope around my hip and headed back down to camp, with Lucille lazily chewing grass and following along behind me.

* * *

In the days and weeks that followed we climbed higher and higher. At 8,800 feet we reached Lyell Valley, then entered narrower and steeper terrain with only an occasional patch of grass and very little or no still water. Waterfalls and steep rapids rushed along beside the trail, and we followed them to high alpine lakes and scattered snowfields. We passed tree line and entered the tundra, where the vegetation is so delicate and tender you could swear you see the footsteps of angels if you only look close enough.

At night after supper, Melva would put a big pot of hot chocolate over the embers to ward away the chill as darkness fell and the temperature dropped. With the last rays of daylight, suddenly the mountaintop above us would burst into bright red alpenglow, fading just as quickly as it appeared.

In that dry, thin, cold air the stars soon filled the sky, so bright we could hardly believe it. Of all the moments of inspiration in the mountains, this is the one your mind reproduces most often: when you're anywhere else on this earth, you look up at the stars and your entire being flashes back to that cold night on the rooftop of the world when the stars were so close they brushed your fingertips.

* * *

We hiked and fished, swam in cold lakes, picnicked in meadows dotted with wildflowers, and slept next to rushing streams. I built fires of green wood to fight off clouds of mosquitos, and Melva killed a rattlesnake that crossed our path. Some mornings we woke to find our tent covered in frost. That same afternoon the intense solar radiation would burn our faces if it weren't for the big-brimmed hats we all wore. On July 8, Melva made Beth a birthday cake over our campfire to celebrate her fifteenth birthday. The girls laughed and played, slept soundly and woke ready to hike alongside our faithful mule, splashed in hot springs and, finally, stood on top of Mount Whitney, admiring the view. As we looked back on where we'd been from that mountaintop vantage, we realized this trip had changed us. Flowers and rainbows had a deeper color, our minds were clearer and our bodies stronger, and we knew that if we could do this—hike 330 miles through the wilderness—we could do anything.

At our last camp, the night before we walked out, I noticed Beth was off by herself, sitting on a big rock. It looked like she was crying. I went over and asked her what the matter was. "I don't want to leave the mountains," she said. This young woman who hadn't wanted to come on our trip before it began now couldn't bear to leave.

Throughout our hike, Beth, Marsha, and Tina Gale kept a journal. On the last page is a poem commemorating our trip. Its last lines read:

> *We have felt the rhythm of the trail for endless miles.*
> *We have walked on the high mountains where trees*
> *cannot grow.*
> *We have stood atop the tallest mountain.*
> *Yet we were never sick and we were never afraid …*
> *Following a mule,*
> *Following a man of the mountains, and*
> *Following a lady of unearthly grace.*

CHAPTER 11

Epiphany

Admiring the hand-carved walking stick perched against the wall of my office more than thirty-five years later, I still remember those days in the High Sierra vividly, as if they happened yesterday. Early in the hike, Tina had picked up the stick on the trail, and each night while we sat around the fire I'd carve patterns on it for her. By the end of the trip, the entire stick was covered with animals and flowers and mountain scenes. It was one of a host of wonderful memories we'd created as a family.

Life between that day and this had been good. I'd spent three and a half decades as a teacher, in both traditional schools and in nature's classroom, as a park ranger. After decades of living in Baytown, Melva and I sold our home and moved to Salida, Colorado, where for eight years we owned and operated an Ace Hardware before I returned to teaching, this time at Salida's Kesner Junior High. In the summers, I worked as a park service interpreter in Rocky Mountain National Park. When it came time to retire in 1995, we chose the small mountain town of Grand Lake, Colorado, at the park's southwestern entrance.

Looking around my lower-level office, more memories from the past cluttered my vision and my mind. Antique clocks, phones from the 1920s, model airplanes, and an entire wall of rocks and fossils filled my private museum. There were pictures of old cars, the smiling faces of my girls, and places around the country that Melva and I had visited. In the center sat a modern computer and on the floor nearby, a trashcan overflowing with paper. You could assume that the person who used this office lived as deeply in the past as he does in the present. And, with one whiff, you could also guess that he sipped Community Coffee, a dark Cajun roast from Louisiana.

In retirement I turned to what some might think is an unlikely hobby for a person who struggles with words. I began to write. I enjoy putting my thoughts to paper, even though it's a real challenge for me. Though words will never flow freely from my thoughts to the computer screen, I have always had imagination, passion, and stories to tell. Writing is also a release. It has given me a chance to correct unresolved problems, discover new unknowns, revisit battles won and lost, and understand and forgive myself and others.

It was on one dark winter morning in December 2003 while writing that something remarkable happened. I had been down in my office since I woke at 5:00 that morning. The lone window in my lower-level retreat let in very little light, and I could just make out the silhouettes of occasional snowflakes floating down from a windless sky. I decided I needed a break and a fresh cup of coffee, so I climbed the stairs to find Melva watching television. Without taking her eyes off the screen, she told me, "Sit down and watch this show. You really need to see this."

As I sat down in my recliner I had no idea what the next moments would bring. In them, I would finally come to understand the painful thorn that had been firmly wedged in my side since my youth. I was about to discover the roots of my inability to read.

* * *

The program was a documentary about Charles Schwab and his lifelong struggle with dyslexia. Though I had heard this word before, I had never really known what it meant. As we sat there watching, the definition became clear. It meant me. Charles Schwab couldn't read, just like me.

I was frozen to my seat. Neither Melva nor I said a word.

As the program unfolded, I began to understand that though our lives were very different, Charles Schwab and I had experienced many of the same things. Growing up in the forties and fifties, he knew from a young age that he was different from the other children. They read with ease while he struggled, having to sound out each word to get its meaning. He had a hard time answering questions about what he'd just read. Writing was a terrible chore. So he kept this all a secret, and focused his energy on other things.

Like me, Charles Schwab was athletic, good at math and science, and outgoing. He got into Stanford because he excelled at golf. Once there, he majored in economics—but English and foreign-language classes were a humiliation. He flunked English twice, then finally passed on the third try. In French, he got an F. When his homework assignment was to memorize a passage from Chaucer, he couldn't get past the first four words.

"When I came out of public high school I thought I could charm my teachers," he said. "I found out in college I couldn't." It was like hearing my own thoughts come out of somebody else's mouth. "That's me," I kept whispering to myself. "That's me."

But there was a larger lesson to this story. Instead of letting his handicap debilitate him, Charles Schwab figured out what he could do well, and he began to work really hard at it. He earned his degree in economics, and then went on to get an MBA, also at Stanford. He started a discount brokerage firm in the 1970s. His company grew and grew because of a special ability Schwab had: he could see solutions to complicated problems before others could; he actually visualized outcomes before they were apparent to anyone else.

I thought back to my days in college and graduate school when I knew what my science professors were going to say before it was out of their mouths. I remembered the debates I'd had with my chemistry professor, and how I was chosen to be a lab assistant for a thermodynamics course even though I'd never studied that field of science. I remembered the ease with which I discussed complex ideas with fellow graduate students and how I loved to show my students the beauty of science and the natural world.

I also thought about those painful days in the fourth grade when I had finally learned to read a few words and scribble out a sentence or two. How I could never read anything that was long, not even a newspaper article, and how I refused to read out loud in front of others.

Here was a man I admired, someone I knew to be extremely intelligent and successful, with whom I'd invested my own money for more than fifteen years. And we shared this. We shared dyslexia.

* * *

From that day forward, for several weeks, I became obsessed with learning more. As soon as the program was over I descended to my office, Googled how to spell *dyslexia*, and started to read. Hours and days passed, and I hardly left my chair. All the other things that were important in my daily life fell away: Rotary Club, my participation in the Chamber of Commerce and the town board, even physical needs like sleep and food. Melva sensed what was happening to me and shared my curiosity and deep emotions as only a wife of fifty years could. Every hour or so she would come downstairs and deliver a small snack or something to drink. I was so engrossed in learning more about dyslexia, I hardly noticed her. Once, when I had been sitting in front of my computer for hours, Melva came down to check on me and said in a firm voice, "Hey, Wrinkle Butt, when are you going to come upstairs and take a break?" I smiled and patted her arm, then turned back to the call of my glowing screen.

The reality of finally knowing was almost more than I could contain. Every symptom associated with dyslexia was one I had experienced many, many times. Finally, I understood. Finally, all the frustrations and struggles I'd felt all my life when it came to reading and writing made sense. I wasn't lazy or slow. I wasn't less than other people. There was a physical, logical reason for my secret, and there was no shame in it.

I printed out folders of information from endless websites, carefully reading each page for more details. Sometimes I'd wake up at 3:00 in the morning, a new thought surfacing, and I just had to slip out of bed to investigate it before it disappeared into the recesses of my mind. Having a name for my problem, something I could research and understand, was an epiphany. In fact, I would even sneak short notes to myself during church.

Normally I am a very social person, but this was a private time, because few people could understand what this revelation meant to me. Melva, a few family members, and a handful of very close friends were the only ones who were aware or even suspected that I was a poor reader. Because of fears of rejection and embarrassment, I had kept this demoralizing secret close to my chest my entire life. Now that I was finally coming to discover why I couldn't read like everyone else, I needed solitude and the love, friendship, and support of the one person who knows me best: my beloved wife.

After days of research, I moved from gathering information to releasing my emotions about it on paper. Everything I wrote I took upstairs and read to Melva. Sometimes it was difficult to say out loud what I had written—years of struggle and pain were deeply tied to how I felt about myself when it came to reading, and now I could finally let that go. As I read to my wife, my throat would tighten and I had to stop and take a deep breath. Tears of relief and joy filled my eyes. My voice shook with emotion.

I decided I wanted to get tested so I could know for sure. So at the age of seventy, I underwent an in-depth educational diagnostic evaluation at Southwest Counseling Associates in Littleton, Colorado. The waiting room was filled with young children and anxious mothers. They glanced at my gray hair, and must have assumed Melva and I were there with a grandchild—until the receptionist called my name and I followed her back to the exam room.

The battery of tests lasted all day, and I was given all the time I needed to finish the parts that required reading. I was a little anxious, but not nervous. There was a sense of peace that what I was doing would finally produce answers that were long overdue.

When the results came a few weeks later, my doctor told me he had discovered my problem. On a scale of one to ten, with ten being the most severe form of dyslexia, I had scored a ten. I had a major cognitive language disability that limited my word recognition skills. The results of the tests put me at a fourth-grade reading level.

My doctor asked me how, with such severe dyslexia, I had managed to teach aircraft mechanics in the military, earn college and graduate-level degrees, and teach science for thirty-five years. I explained my ability to think in pictures, to visualize solutions to problems easily, and the learning system I had used throughout college and graduate school. He listened, nodding.

"That makes sense," he told me, "because in addition to your dyslexia, you also have a very high IQ. It's not an unusual situation that people with learning disabilities have a high intellectual capacity to compensate for their inability to do things like read or write. The brain finds other ways to allow people to accomplish things. You are a remarkable example."

So I finally had my answer. It felt as though a huge weight had been lifted off my shoulders. One small word, dyslexia, changed everything.

I felt like I had been given a new life.

CHAPTER 12
Accepted

It was a typical morning in Grand Lake, Colorado. As happened most days, a group of us old-timers were meeting for coffee at the Hub Bakery to solve the world's problems. On cue, in walked the town manager, Shane Hale, and we immediately began running him through the gauntlet in our joking manner. Laughing, he finally yielded. "Who do you think I am, a Mensa?" he asked. "Definitely not," a buddy teased, and Shane went on his way.

That word, *Mensa*, struck a chord in my memory. Five years earlier I'd heard it, when my doctor at Southwest Counseling Associates was going over my test results. He'd explained that although I had a major cognitive learning deficit that limited my ability to read and spell, the test that measured my innate intelligence showed that I was in the superior range—within the top 1 percent of the general population. "These results would qualify you for Mensa," he'd said. Not knowing what that meant, I simply took it as a compliment and stored the word away.

But Shane's joking outburst made me curious. As I walked home from the bakery, I kept thinking about Mensa, and when I got home I searched the Internet to find out what it was.

The first thing I discovered after reading that Mensa is a society for bright people from every walk of life was that the only qualification for membership is to score in the 98th percentile or above on an approved intelligence test. The test I'd taken, the Wechsler Adult Intelligence Scale, was one, and it showed I'd scored in the 99.6th percentile.

The idea that I qualified for Mensa stunned me. Could it possibly be that I could be accepted into a society for people with high intelligence? Who did I think I was? I kept reading and thinking, then spoke with a friend of mine in Grand Lake about it. "You have nothing to apologize for," he said. "Intelligence isn't a bad word. I think you should apply." He was right. I didn't have to convince myself or anyone else that I was worthy. I was okay as I was, dyslexia and all—more than okay, in fact.

The next step was to call the American Mensa office in Arlington, Texas, to find out more. The woman on the other end of the phone was very interested in me; we talked for at least thirty minutes. I told her I was a poor reader, but she didn't seem to care about that at all. Instead, she wanted to know how I thought, what my interests were, and what fields of science most intrigued me. "Do you enjoy working by yourself?" she asked. When I said yes, I always had, she encouraged me even more. "You really should apply," she said.

As soon as we got off the phone I downloaded the application. It was very involved. It took me about three weeks to provide all the information they requested. But I did, including the original copy of my Wechsler intelligence test. Then I typed up my cover letter. The first part explained all my educational and career achievements. The second part said this:

Now that I have given you some of my background, may I tell you who I really am?

I have always had difficulty with reading, spelling, and grammar, but I never let that stop me and I never understood why until I was 70 years old.

When I was in public school in the forties and college in the fifties, the word "dyslexia" was never used. It was not until 2004 that I realized that cognitive language dysfunction might be my problem. I located Southwest Counseling Associates in Denver and arranged for an evaluation.

In the evaluation I scored low in things that were evaluated by reading and language, however for the things that were evaluated without reading, I scored high.

In public school, I was a poor student and was unable to read, write, or spell with any confidence, an inability that put me in good company. A teacher of Albert Einstein wrote that he was a very poor student and that he was mentally slow; a teacher of Louisa May Alcott said she would never be able to write anything for popular consumption; a teacher of Thomas Edison said that it was useless for him to attend school any longer.

I am in no way implying that I am on their level, but we do share common inabilities in our early education.

I am enclosing a copy of the Confidential Educational Diagnostic Evaluation performed on

January 14, 2004, for your evaluation. Based on the enclosed information, I would respectfully request that I be approved as a member of The American Mensa.

Three weeks went by and I didn't hear a thing. My son-in-law and the friend I'd told about applying to Mensa continued to encourage me, but I knew I should try to stop thinking about whether or not I would get in and just enjoy the wonderful life Melva and I had built for ourselves.

Then, on September 1, 2009, an email came:

Dear Glenn,

I am honored to welcome you as the newest member of the American Mensa Society.

When I realized what the email said, everything started to slow down. I sat for a while, and then I read it again. I felt like I had just won the lottery in life. I closed my eyes, bowed my head, and felt thankful for being recognized as someone I never considered myself to be. The coat of low self-esteem I had worn most of my life was finally loosening. I could almost feel it fall to the floor.

* * *

A small amount of recognition goes a long way in making a lonely person a hero.

As I sat in front of my computer for a few more minutes, emotions from deep inside started coming to the surface, filling my eyes and tightening my throat. My very next thought was "Where's Melva?"

I'm not the type of person to holler and run through the house with good news. Instead, I quietly found my wife, showed her the incredible news, and we shared a long, emotional embrace, both of us feeling the impact this would have and the positive change it would bring to both our lives.

After enjoying this news privately for a few days, my next step was to write a letter to my closest friends and family. I titled it "A Journey Ends." The last paragraph went like this:

> To my friends and family, I am and will be the same person I have always been, but to me, the knowledge of my dyslexia and being accepted to the America Mensa has brought a peace and self-confidence that I have never had before. It truly validates who I am and gives me a better understanding of the journey I have traveled to get where I am today. The greatest asset and traveling partner on this journey is my wife, Melva. Without her, the journey would not have been possible, and surely the destination would have been different.

The reaction to my letter and to conversations with close friends was interesting. People just couldn't seem to understand how important this achievement was to me. One of my friends said, "I think you're overstating the importance of the situation." I was stunned. To me, that was impossible. Others offered support with "We always knew" or "That doesn't surprise me"—kind words that didn't reflect the enormous accomplishment being accepted into Mensa represented for me. When I brought it up in future conversations, talk would quickly turn to everyday matters, making it hit home how difficult it was for others to walk in my shoes. They truly could not know what it meant to be a nonreader in a world of words—and for that I couldn't blame them.

And that was when I decided to write this book.

* * *

Henry Ford said, "One of the greatest discoveries a man makes, one of the greatest surprises, is to find he can do what he was afraid he couldn't do." That is what this book represents for me. It shows that I am able to do something I never imagined I could do. And it proves that if you set your mind to something and are willing to work long and hard enough to finish the task, you can do it.

As I look back at the words I have struggled to put down, I realize that writing this book is more than just putting my life story on paper. Along the way, I have rediscovered myself, and all of the people who made my journey possible.

In these pages I see myself as a little boy who found peace and happiness in the natural world. At an early age, he faced his fears and struggled to fit in at school and at home—and succeeded in making friends and finding acceptance. His grandparents helped him discover who he was in his teens by encouraging the self-confidence he would need to mature into a young man. In high school he met the love of his life, a woman who would support him through six decades of marriage, provide him with a beautiful family, and never waver in her love for him, just as he never wavers in his devotion to her. The Air Force set the young man's path to becoming a teacher in motion, and college taught him that with hard work and dedication he could succeed. By the time he began his career and went to graduate school, he knew he was put on this earth to be a teacher and a scientist.

Then, at age seventy, the answer to a lifelong question finally found him. He discovered he had dyslexia. Being accepted to the American Mensa six years later gave him one more gift: peace.

And now his story, my story, is in your hands. The very thing I have covered up all my life has been uncovered. The entire world can read these words and get a glimpse into my life.

I have moved beyond the grace of silence and discovered the energy of truth.

Epilogue

Everyone has a different idea of what they would like to do when they get to heaven—assuming, of course, that that is where they're headed.

Some people want to sit on a cloud and play a harp. Others want to meet Jesus or have a talk with John the Baptist. Many look forward to seeing their mother or dad, a lost child or dear friend.

I have something different in mind. When I get to heaven, I want to read a book. And not just to myself—I want to read it out loud, in front of an audience.

Being a primary dyslexic, I have never been able to take apart the sounds that make up words, blend them to form new expressions, or analyze their pieces to understand their meaning. And I have never, ever read out loud in public.

So that is my wish.

When I finish, I will close the book, look around at my listeners, and say, "Now I know I am in heaven."

About the Author

Glenn Harrington grew up on a small farm in Baytown, Texas, the third of three sons born to an itinerate preacher. He joined the Air Force at the height of the Korean War, and entered Midwestern University on the GI Bill in 1954. Glenn holds a bachelor's degree in geology and a master's degree in natural science. He taught science in public schools for 35 years and worked as a naturalist for the National Park Service for 11 summers.

Glenn and his loving wife, Melva, recently celebrated 61 years of marriage. In 2009, at the age of 76, Glenn was accepted to the American Mensa Society.